AN

UNCOMMON SCOLD

COMPILED BY

Abby Adams

A FIRESIDE BOOK
Published by Simon & Schuster
New York London Toronto Sydney Tokyo Singapore

FIRESIDE
Rockefeller Center
1230 Avenue of the Americas
New York, New York 10020

First Fireside Edition 1994

FIRESIDE and colophon are
registered trademarks of Simon & Schuster Inc.

Designed by Edith Fowler
Manufactured in the United States of America

10 9 8 7 6 5 4 3 2 1

Library of Congress Cataloging in Publication Data

An Uncommon scold.

1. Women—Quotations.   I. Adams, Abby.
PN6084.W65U5   1989   082′.082   89-21885
ISBN 0-671-69022-1
ISBN 0-671-88526-X Pbk.

Contents

Introduction

by DONALD E. WESTLAKE

What is a common scold? It's a criminal offense. According to Sir William Blackstone, the eighteenth-century British jurist, "a common scold—'communis rixatrix'—(for our law Latin confines it to the feminine gender) is a public nuisance." Jacob's Law Dictionary defines it further: "Scolds, in a legal sense, are troublesome and angry women, who, by their brawling and wrangling amongst their neighbors, break the public peace."

A *common scold* was a crime, in other words, that consisted essentially of speaking one's mind, and a crime that only a woman could commit. The punishment was a public ducking, in a ducking stool plunged into some handy body of cold water.

It's wonderful how far civilization has advanced since those olden days. Why, the last time a woman was indicted as a common scold in the United States was way back in 1971.

1971? Yes. That was, in fact, a full four years after the crime of common scold had been declared obsolete in Great Britain by the Criminal Law Act 1967. But Great Britain is not New 9

Jersey, where, in 1971, Marion B. Dunlevy was arrested, fingerprinted, and indicted as a common scold after an argument with two (male) neighbors over a parked car. The State Superior Court threw the case out the following year, but the law is on the books. So watch it.

The last woman *convicted* of being a common scold in the United States was a journalist named Ann Royall, who in 1829 ran afoul of a fundamentalist minister with political ambitions named . . . uh, let me see. That one was named Ezra Stiles Ely, and among the things Ann Royall said about Ely and his group was that they were "morticians . . . hoping to preside at the death of the Constitution." Ely's followers brought the charge of common scold against Ms. Royall in the state of Maryland, and a jury there found her guilty. Her attorney appealed, asking for a reversal on the basis that the only punishment ever prescribed for a common scold was ducking, that ducking had never been practiced in the United States, that ducking would be a cruel and unusual punishment and so unconstitutional, that the crime therefore had no punishment, and that a crime without a punishment ceases to exist. (The legal mind never ceases to amuse.)

The appeal was denied, Judge Cranch—yes, Judge Cranch—writing, "If a part of the common-law punishment of the offence has become obsolete, the only effect is, that the discretion of the court is so far limited. The offence is not obsolete, and cannot become obsolete so long as a common scold is a common nuisance."

The offence is not obsolete. So watch it.

10   Judge Cranch fined Ann Royall ten bucks, and she went

back to work denouncing Ely. And in 1986, in a nice postscript, Marion Dunlevy, her descendant-in-crime in New Jersey, published a biography of Ann Royall, written with Alice S. Maxwell, in which they comment on their subject's current obscurity: "It was left to the important men in her life (the politicians whose cause she had defended) to celebrate her . . . not many did, for men do not celebrate women if they don't have to." Clearly, Ann Royall had a mouth on her, and so do Marion Dunlevy and Alice Maxwell.

That's the mark of the common scold, right there. Her smarting victim can almost always be heard to mutter, while slinking away, "She's got a mouth on her, that one." And so she does. And so, for quite a long time, women were not supposed to.

Which brings us to the uncommon scold, the woman who considers that to have a mouth on her is a mark of independence, intelligence, pride, and wit. I have the good fortune to be closely related to one such, Abby Adams, who has collected herein a bouquet of the best that mouthy women down the ages have had to say on every subject under the sun.

Abby has not been preachy or one-sided or political in putting this book together, but has let women have their say in as great a variety as they might wish: Margaret Thatcher and Jane Fonda are both here, as are Ayn Rand and Germaine Greer, Anita Bryant and Rita Mae Brown, Nancy Reagan and Emma Goldman, Marie Antoinette and Bella Abzug, plus the Dickinsons, Angie and Emily, and the Mansfields, Katherine and Jayne. Madame de Staël and Countess Tolstoy and Czarina Alexandra mix more or less comfortably with Janis Joplin and Golda Meir and Moms Mabley. And Abby has sorted the 11 great variety of their utterances into every subject you can think of—except professional sports. No, come to think of it, Billie Jean King is here as well, with a sports tip.

When I was asked to be the only male voice among this monstrous regiment of women I suspected a trap. Were they waiting for me to act *like a man?* Maybe I'd do a hearty and patronizing piece, full of jolly humor at the level of sayings found on barbecue aprons, with some manly pats on the head all round. No, wait; pats on the fanny, I believe it's called. (Imagine patting Elizabeth I on the fanny; that's the last you'd see of *that* hand.)

Or maybe I'd do a mea culpa piece, taking on the accumulated guilt of untold generations of oppressors with muttonchop whiskers, and volunteering to do three or four years' worth of household chores in atonement. Mmm; maybe not.

Alternatively, I could do a defensive piece, the whine of *Why are they picking on us?* lightly concealed by nervous giggling: "Move over, Rodney Dangerfield! *None* of us gets any respect!"

Sorry; I can't do any of that. This is supposed to be an introduction, so that's what I'll do. May I have the pleasure of introducing you to a terrific book compiled by a terrific person, and containing in easy-to-digest capsule form the very best of the feminine mind.

I like to look at women, you know. I like to listen to women, too. Listen.

Acting ————————

Acting is the most minor of gifts and not a very high-class way to earn a living. After all, Shirley Temple could do it at the age of four.

KATHARINE HEPBURN

When I cry, do you want the tears to run all the way or shall I stop halfway down?

MARGARET O'BRIEN
(at age six)

Acting is like painting pictures on bathroom tissues. Ten minutes later you throw them away and they're gone.

SHELLEY WINTERS 13

Acting is standing up naked and turning around very slowly.

ROSALIND RUSSELL

The important thing in acting is to be able to laugh and cry. If I have to cry, I think of my sex life. If I have to laugh, I think of my sex life.

GLENDA JACKSON

I mean, the question actors most often get asked is how they can bear saying the same things over and over again night after night, but God knows the answer to *that* is, don't we all *anyway;* might as well get paid for it.

ELAINE DUNDY

The stage is actor's country. You have to get your passport stamped every so often or they take away your citizenship.

VANESSA REDGRAVE

You can do what you like in Shakespeare because people don't understand half of it anyway. But you can't in an Irish play because it really means what it says.

SIOBHAN MCKENNA

Every actor has a natural animosity toward every other actor, present or absent, living or dead.

LOUISE BROOKS

An actor can remember his briefest notice well into senescence and long after he has forgotten his phone number and where he lives.

JEAN KERR 15

What acting means is that you've got to get out of your own skin.

KATHARINE HEPBURN

What you get is a living—what you give is a life.

LILLIAN GISH

Aging ━━━━━━━━━━

The years that a woman subtracts from her age are not lost. They are added to other women's.

DIANE DE POITIERS

From birth to age 18, a girl needs good parents, from 18 to 35 she needs good looks, from 35 to 55 she needs a good personality, and from 55 on she needs cash.

SOPHIE TUCKER

A woman is as young as her knees.

MARY QUANT

The secret of staying young is to live honestly, eat slowly, and lie about your age.

LUCILLE BALL

When a woman reaches twenty-six in America, she's on the slide. It's downhill all the way from then on. It doesn't give you a tremendous feeling of confidence and well-being.

LAUREN BACALL

Strength of body, and that character of countenance which the French term *physionomie,* women do not acquire before thirty, any more than men.

MARY WOLLSTONECRAFT

Preparing for the worst is an activity I have taken up since I turned thirty-five, and the worst actually began to happen.

DELIA EPHRON 17

The lovely thing about being forty is that you can appreciate twenty-five-year-old men more.

COLLEEN MCCULLOUGH

> Youth is a silly, vapid state;
> Old age with fears and ills is rife;
> This simple boon I beg of Fate—
> A thousand years of Middle Life!

CAROLYN WELLS

All one's life as a young woman one is on show, a focus of attention, people notice you. You set yourself up to be noticed and admired. And then, not expecting it, you become middle-aged and anonymous. No one notices you. You achieve a wonderful freedom. It is a positive thing. You can move about, unnoticed and invisible.

DORIS LESSING

I have everything now I had twenty years ago—except now it's all lower.

GYPSY ROSE LEE

The post-office has a great charm at one period of our lives. When you have lived to my age, you will begin to think letters are never worth going through the rain for.

JANE AUSTEN

I refuse to admit I'm more than fifty-two even if that does make my sons illegitimate.

NANCY, LADY ASTOR

I'd like to go on being thirty-five for a long time.

MARGARET THATCHER
(at age fifty-four)

You know, when I first went into the movies Lionel Barrymore played my grandfather. Later he played my father and finally he played my husband. If he had lived, I'm sure I would have played his mother. That's the way it is in Hollywood. The men get younger and the women get older.

LILLIAN GISH

I wish it were OK in this country to look one's age, whatever it is. Maturity has a lot going for it, even in terms of esthetics. For example, you no longer get bubblegum stuck in your braces.

CYRA McFADDEN

. . . as I must leave off being young, I find many Douceurs in being a sort of Chaperon, for I am put on the Sofa near the fire & can drink as much wine as I like.

JANE AUSTEN 19

The hardest years in life are those between ten and seventy.

HELEN HAYES
(at age eighty-three)

America

In the United States there is more space where nobody is than where anybody is. That is what makes America what it is.

GERTRUDE STEIN

Europeans used to say Americans were puritanical. Then they discovered that we were not puritans. So now they say we are obsessed with sex.

MARY MCCARTHY

In America sex is an obsession, in other parts of the world it is a fact.

MARLENE DIETRICH

American men say "I love you" as part of the conversation.

LIV ULLMANN

When an American heiress wants to buy a man, she at once crosses the Atlantic.

MARY MCCARTHY

Things on the whole are much faster in America; people don't *stand for election,* they *run for office.* If a person says he's sick, it doesn't mean regurgitating, it means *ill. Mad* means angry, not insane. Don't ask for the left-luggage; it's called a check-room. A nice joint means a good pub, not roast meat.

JESSICA MITFORD

Those who sit in a glass house do wrong to throw stones about them; besides, the American glass house is rather thin, it will break easily, and the interior is anything but a gainly sight.

EMMA GOLDMAN

To be a celebrity in America is to be forgiven everything.

MARY MCGRORY

Anatomy ─────────

Really that little dealybob is too far away from the hole. It should be built right in.

LORETTA LYNN
(on the female body)

Woman has ovaries, a uterus . . . It is often said that she thinks with her glands. Man superbly ignores the fact that his anatomy also includes glands, such as the testicles, and that they secrete hormones.

SIMONE DE BEAUVOIR

If women are supposed to be less rational and more emotional at the beginning of our menstrual cycle when the female hormone is at its lowest level, then why isn't it logical to say that, in those few days, women behave the most like the way men behave all month long?

GLORIA STEINEM 23

A full bosom is actually a millstone around a woman's neck; it endears her to the men who want to make their mammet of her, but she is never allowed to think that their popping eyes actually see her.

GERMAINE GREER

Ladies, here's a hint; if you're playing against a friend who has big boobs, bring her to the net and make her hit backhand volleys. That's the hardest shot for the well-endowed. "I've got to hit over them or under them, but I can't hit through," Annie Jones used to always moan to me. Not having much in my bra, I found it hard to sympathize with her.

BILLIE JEAN KING

It's impossible to be more flat-chested than I am.

CANDICE BERGEN

Animals

If a fish is the movement of water embodied, given shape, then a cat is a diagram and pattern of subtle air.

DORIS LESSING

I suspect that many an ailurophobe hates cats only because he feels they are better than he is—more honest, more secure, more loved, more whatever he is not.

WINIFRED CARRIERE

The playful kitten with its pretty little tigerish gambole is infinitely more amusing than half the people one is obliged to live with in the world.

LADY SYDNEY MORGAN

Some people say that cats are sneaky, evil, and cruel. True, and they have many other fine qualities as well.

MISSY DIZICK 25

Let us love dogs, let us only love dogs! Men and cats are unworthy creatures.

MARIA KONSTANTINOVA BASHKIRTSEFF

The more I see of men, the more I like dogs.

MADAME DE STAËL

So many get reformed through religion. I got reformed through dogs. I underwent menopause without taking even an aspirin, because I was so busy whelping puppies. Dogs saved my life. I recommend having four-legged animals to cure the mid-life crisis.

LINA BASQUETTE

Don't make the mistake of treating your dogs like humans, or they'll treat you like dogs.

MARTHA SCOTT

Some of my best leading men have been dogs and horses.

ELIZABETH TAYLOR

Architecture

Washington is an endless series of mock palaces clearly built for clerks.

ADA LOUISE HUXTABLE

In my experience, if you have to keep the lavatory door shut by extending your left leg, it's modern architecture.

NANCY BANKS SMITH 27

Art ━━━━━━━━━━━━━━━

Religion and art spring from the same root and are close kin.
Economics and art are strangers.

WILLA CATHER

No artist is ahead of his time. He *is* his time. It is just that
the others are behind the time.

MARTHA GRAHAM

I longed to arrest all beauty that came before me, and at length
the longing has been satisfied.

JULIA MARGARET CAMERON

A photograph is a secret about a secret. The more it tells you
the less you know.

DIANE ARBUS

One thing I learned above all else from Margaret Bourke-White is the kind of woman I didn't want to be.

PEGGY SARGENT
(her secretary)

It gave me great pleasure to think that I could take wood, make it good, and make people like Rockefeller buy it with paper money.

LOUISE NEVELSON 29

Aren't the artists brave to go out and paint a sea as rough as that? . . . I don't see how he kept his canvas dry.

RUTH DRAPER
(at an art exhibition in Boston)

If Michelangelo painted in Caesar's Palace, would that make it any less art?

CHER

He is a delightful, kindly, friendly, simple little man, and one would know him for a great man anywhere. At the moment, he was extremely excited and overjoyed because his mother-in-law had just died . . . and he was looking forward to the funeral.

DAME EDITH SITWELL
(on meeting Picasso)

I don't much enjoy looking at paintings in general. I know too much about them. I take them apart.

GEORGIA O'KEEFFE

Why should I paint dead fish, onions and beer glasses? Girls are so much prettier.

MARIE LAURENCIN

Attraction _____

One of the paramount reasons for staying attractive is so you can have somebody to go to bed with.

HELEN GURLEY BROWN

My husband said he wanted to have a relationship with a redhead, so I dyed my hair red.

JANE FONDA

Men ought to be more conscious of their bodies as an object of delight.

GERMAINE GREER

Sex appeal is 50 percent what you've got and 50 percent what people think you've got.

SOPHIA LOREN 31

Boys don't make passes at female smart-asses.

LETTY COTTIN POGREBIN

As I look around the West End these days, it seems to me that outside every thin girl is a fat man, trying to get in.

KATHARINE WHITEHORN

I know there are nights when I have power, when I could put on something and walk in somewhere, and if there is a man who doesn't look at me, it's because he's gay.

KATHLEEN TURNER

Seamed stockings aren't subtle but they certainly do the job. You shouldn't wear them when out with someone you're not prepared to sleep with, since their presence is tantamount to saying, "Hi there, big fellow, please rip my clothes off at your earliest opportunity." If you really want your escort paralytic with lust, stop frequently to adjust the seams.

CYNTHIA HEIMEL

Scheherazade is easy; a little black dress is very difficult.

COCO CHANEL

Authors

It's not a bad idea to get in the habit of writing down one's thoughts. It saves one having to bother anyone with them.

ISABEL COLEGATE

The novelist, afraid his ideas may be foolish, slyly puts them in the mouth of some other fool and reserves the right to disavow them.

DIANE JOHNSON

The best time for planning a book is while you're doing the dishes.

AGATHA CHRISTIE

I've made characters live, so that people talk about them at cocktail parties, and that, to me, is what counts.

JACQUELINE SUSANN 33

My family can always tell when I'm well into a novel because the meals get very crummy.

ANNE TYLER

I wrote the story myself. It's all about a girl who lost her reputation but never missed it.

MAE WEST

I'm a lousy writer; a helluva lot of people have got lousy taste.

GRACE METALIOUS

I no more thought of style or literary excellence than the mother who rushes into the street and cries for help to save her children from a burning house, thinks of the teachings of the rhetorician or the elocutionist.

HARRIET BEECHER STOWE
(*on writing* Uncle Tom's Cabin)

Once the grammar has been learned [writing] is simply talking on paper and in time learning what not to say.

BERYL BAINBRIDGE

I suppose I am a born novelist, for the things that I imagine are more vital and vivid to me than the things I remember.

ELLEN GLASGOW

Looking back, I imagine I was always writing. Twaddle it was too. But better far write twaddle or anything, anything, than nothing at all.

KATHERINE MANSFIELD

Writers should be read, but neither seen nor heard.

DAPHNE DU MAURIER

Beauty ———————————

All God's children are not beautiful. Most of God's children are, in fact, barely presentable.

FRAN LEBOWITZ

There is not one female comic who was beautiful as a little girl.

JOAN RIVERS

Plain women know more about men than beautiful ones do.

KATHARINE HEPBURN

I'm tired of all this nonsense about beauty being only skin-deep. That's deep enough. What do you want—an adorable pancreas?

JEAN KERR

There are no ugly women, only lazy ones.

Any girl can be glamorous. All you have to do is stand still and look stupid.

HEDY LAMARR

Most beautiful but dumb girls think they are smart and get away with it, because other people, on the whole, aren't much smarter.

LOUISE BROOKS

All women think they're ugly, even pretty women. A man who understood this could fuck more women than Don Giovanni. They *all* think their cunts are ugly . . . They all find fault with their figures . . . Even models and actresses, even the women you think are so beautiful that they have nothing to worry about do worry all the time.

ERICA JONG

In my own mind, I am still that fat brunette from Toledo, and I always will be.

GLORIA STEINEM

No one ever called me pretty when I was a little girl.

MARILYN MONROE

Can you imagine anybody wanting to look this way for real?

DOLLY PARTON

It's not what you'd call a figure, is it?

TWIGGY

It is eleven years since I have seen my figure in a glass. The last reflection I saw there was so disagreeable, I resolved to spare myself such mortification in the future.

LADY MARY WORTLEY MONTAGU

Circumstances alter faces.

CAROLYN WELLS

I shall never get used to not being the most beautiful woman in the room. It was an intoxication to sweep in and know every man had turned his head. It kept me in form.

LADY RANDOLPH CHURCHILL
(JENNIE)

Vanity, like murder, will out.

HANNAH COWLEY 39

California ──────────

California: The west coast of Iowa.

JOAN DIDION

The trouble with Oakland is that when you get there, there isn't any there there.

GERTRUDE STEIN

As one went to Europe to see the living past, so one must visit Southern California to observe the future.

ALISON LURIE

All creative people should be required to leave California for three months every year.

GLORIA SWANSON

Pick your enemies carefully or you'll never make it in Los Angeles.

RONA BARRETT

The people are unreal. The flowers are unreal, they don't smell. The fruit is unreal, it doesn't taste of anything. The whole place is a glaring, gaudy, nightmarish set, built up in the desert.

ETHEL BARRYMORE
(on first arriving in Hollywood, 1932)

I'm not a little girl from a little town making good in a big town. I'm a big girl from a big town making good in a little town.

MAE WEST
(arriving in Hollywood)

What I like about Hollywood is that one can get along by knowing two words of English—swell and lousy.

VICKI BAUM

Living in Hollywood is like living in a lit cigar butt.

PHYLLIS DILLER 41

Hollywood—an emotional Detroit.

LILLIAN GISH

Hollywood's a place where they'll pay you a thousand dollars for a kiss, and fifty cents for your soul.

MARILYN MONROE

Canada

Canada is useful only to provide me with furs.

MADAME DE POMPADOUR

42

Children _____

An ugly baby is a very nasty object, and the prettiest is frightful when undressed.

QUEEN VICTORIA

I blame Rousseau, myself. "Man is born free", indeed. Man is not born free, he is born attached to his mother by a cord and is not capable of looking after himself for at least seven years (seventy in some cases).

KATHARINE WHITEHORN

I love children, especially when they cry, for then someone takes them away.

NANCY MITFORD

Children make the most desirable opponents in Scrabble as they are both easy to beat and fun to cheat.

FRAN LEBOWITZ

Thank God kids never mean well.

LILY TOMLIN 43

The real menace in dealing with a five-year-old is that in no time at all you begin to sound like a five-year-old.

JEAN KERR

Ask your child what he wants for dinner only if he's buying.

FRAN LEBOWITZ

I read one psychologist's theory that said, "Never strike a child in anger." When could I strike him? When he is kissing me on my birthday? When he is recuperating from measles? Do I slap the Bible out of his hand on a Sunday?

ERMA BOMBECK

I know I was cruel to other children because I remember stuffing their nostrils with putty, and beating a little boy with stinging nettles.

VITA SACKVILLE-WEST

Whimpy, little Whimpy,
    Cried so much one day,
His grandma couldn't stand it,
    And his mother ran away.

MARY MAPES DODGE

The fussed shall be last, and the last shall be fussed.

LADY AGNES JEKYLL

Remember that as a teenager you are at the last stage in your life when you will be happy to hear that the phone is for you.

FRAN LEBOWITZ 45

Never lend your car to anyone to whom you have given birth.

ERMA BOMBECK

[A successful parent is one] who raises a child who grows up and is able to pay for her or his own psychoanalysis.

NORA EPHRON

If you have never been hated by your child, you have never been a parent.

BETTE DAVIS

You can get used to anything if you have to, even to feeling perpetually guilty.

GOLDA MEIR
(on her inattention to her children)

Sometimes when I look at my children I say to myself, "Lillian, you should have stayed a virgin."

LILLIAN CARTER

Conception

Women who miscalculate are called "mothers."

ABIGAIL VAN BUREN

Men do not think of sons and daughters, when they fall in love.

ELIZABETH BARRETT BROWNING

It serves me right for putting all my eggs in one bastard.

DOROTHY PARKER
(upon entering the hospital to have an abortion)

Some men are so macho they'll get you pregnant just to kill a rabbit.

MAUREEN MURPHY 47

. . . the male function is to produce sperm. We now have sperm banks.

VALERIE SOLANIS

No test tube can breed love and affection. No frozen packet of semen ever read a story to a sleepy child.

SHIRLEY WILLIAMS

If I had a cock for a day I would get myself pregnant.

GERMAINE GREER

If men could get pregnant, abortion would be a sacrament.

FLORYNCE KENNEDY

If pregnancy were a book they would cut the last two chapters.

NORA EPHRON

Culture _____

Culture is an instrument wielded by professors to manufacture professors, who when their turn comes, will manufacture professors.

SIMONE WEIL

All of Stratford, in fact, suggests powdered history—add hot water and stir and you have a delicious, nourishing Shakespeare.

MARGARET HALSEY

One old lady who wants her head lifted wouldn't be so bad, but you multiply her two hundred and fifty thousand times and what you get is a book club.

FLANNERY O'CONNOR

Mrs. Bellinger is one of the ladies who pursue Culture in bands, as though it were dangerous to meet it alone.

EDITH WHARTON

Death —————————————————————

Faith, Sir, we are here today, and gone to-morrow.

APHRA BEHN

Death seems to provide the minds of the Anglo-Saxon race with a greater fund of innocent amusement than any other single subject . . . the tale must be about dead bodies or very wicked people, preferably both, before the Tired Business Man can feel really happy.

DOROTHY L. SAYERS

50 Whenever I prepare for a journey I prepare as for death.

Should I never return, all is in order. This is what life has taught me.

KATHERINE MANSFIELD

If I had any decency, I'd be dead. Most of my friends are.

DOROTHY PARKER
(at age seventy)

I have always admired the Esquimaux. One fine day a delicious meal is cooked for dear old mother, and then she goes walking away over the ice, *and doesn't come back.*

AGATHA CHRISTIE

Death is my neighbor now.

DAME EDITH EVANS
*(in a radio interview,
a week before her death at eighty-eight)*

Goddammit! He beat me to it.

JANIS JOPLIN
(on hearing of Jimi Hendrix's death) 51

Get my Swan costume ready.

ANNA PAVLOVA
(last words)

All my possessions for one moment of time.

ELIZABETH I
(last words)

Worldly faces never look so worldly as at a funeral.

GEORGE ELIOT

O death where is thy sting? O grave where is thy victory? Where, indeed? Many a badly stung survivor, faced with the aftermath of some relative's funeral, has ruefully conceded that the victory has been won hands down by the funeral establishment—in disastrously unequal battle.

JESSICA MITFORD

The tombstone is about the only thing that can stand upright and lie on its face at the same time.

MARY WILSON LITTLE

Death is simply a shedding of the physical body, like the butterfly coming out of a cocoon . . . It's like putting away your winter coat when spring comes.

ELISABETH KÜBLER-ROSS

There will be sex after death, we just won't be able to feel it.

LILY TOMLIN

In heaven they will bore you, in hell you will bore them.

KATHARINE WHITEHORN

Dependence ————————

It is sad that my emotional dependence on the man I love should have killed so much of my energy and ability; there was certainly once a great deal of energy in me.

SONYA TOLSTOY

If I have to lead another life in any of the planets, I shall take precious good care not to hang myself around any man's neck, either as a locket or a millstone.

JANE CARLYLE

It is easier to live through someone else than to become complete yourself.

BETTY FRIEDAN

No one can build his security upon the nobleness of another person.

WILLA CATHER

Diaries

It's the good girls who keep the diaries; the bad girls never have the time.

TALLULAH BANKHEAD

Keep a diary and one day it'll keep you.

MAE WEST

Diet

I've been on a diet for two weeks and all I've lost is two weeks.

TOTIE FIELDS 55

. . . unnecessary dieting is because everything from television to fashion ads has made it seem wicked to cast a shadow. This wild emaciated look appeals to some women, though not to many men, who are seldom seen pinning up a *Vogue* illustration in a machine shop.

PEG BRACKEN

I feel about airplanes the way I feel about diets. It seems to me they are wonderful things for other people to go on.

JEAN KERR

I've been on a constant diet for the last two decades. I've lost a total of 789 pounds. By all accounts, I should be hanging from a charm bracelet.

ERMA BOMBECK

I stay in marvelous shape. I worry it off.

NANCY REAGAN

Where do you go to get anorexia?

SHELLEY WINTERS

Give me a dozen such heart-breaks, if that would help me to lose a couple of pounds.

COLETTE

I had no reason to reform, repent or recant so I simply reduced.

ELIZABETH GURLEY FLYNN
(coming out of prison—at age sixty-seven—
where she had lost seventy-five pounds)

Divorce ━━━━━━━━━━

He's the kind of man a woman would have to marry to get rid of.

MAE WEST

You never really know a man until you have divorced him.

ZSA ZSA GABOR 57

She always believed in the old adage—leave them while you're looking good.

ANITA LOOS

I know one husband and wife who, whatever the official reasons given to the court for the breakup of their marriage, were really divorced because the husband believed that nobody ought to read while he was talking and the wife that nobody ought to talk while she was reading.

VERA BRITTAIN

Being divorced is like being hit by a Mack truck. If you live through it, you start looking very carefully to the right and to the left.

JEAN KERR

When a marriage ends, who is left to understand it?

JOYCE CAROL OATES

Oh, don't worry about Alan . . . Alan will always land on somebody's feet.

DOROTHY PARKER
(on the day her divorce from Alan Campbell became final)

In Biblical times, a man could have as many wives as he could afford. Just like today.

ABIGAIL VAN BUREN

I never took money from anybody in my divorces. I'm psychopathically independent.

LINA BASQUETTE

In our family we don't divorce our men—we bury them.

RUTH GORDON

Education

A good education is usually harmful to a dancer. A good calf is better than a good head.

AGNES DE MILLE 59

The first idea that the child must acquire, in order to be actively disciplined, is that of the difference between good and evil; and the task of the educator lies in seeing that the child does not confound good with immobility and evil with activity, as often happens in the case of oldtime discipline.

MARIA MONTESSORI

Men get opinions as boys learn to spell,
By reiteration chiefly.

ELIZABETH BARRETT BROWNING

Education was almost always a matter of luck—usually ill-luck—in those distant days.

GEORGE ELIOT

Prejudices, it is well known, are most difficult to eradicate from the heart whose soil has never been loosened or fertilized by education; they grow there, firm as weeds among stones.

CHARLOTTE BRONTË

Lack of education is an extraordinary handicap when one is being offensive.

JOSEPHINE TEY

Egotism

He was like a cock who thought the sun had risen to hear him crow.

GEORGE ELIOT

Egotism—usually just a case of mistaken nonentity.

BARBARA STANWYCK 61

Self-love depressed becomes self-loathing.

SALLY KEMPTON

I've never any pity for conceited people, because I think they carry their comfort about with them.

GEORGE ELIOT

How pleasant it is, at the end of the day,
No follies to have to repent;
But reflect on the past, and be able to say,
That my time has been properly spent.

JANE TAYLOR

Enemies

To have a good enemy, choose a friend: he knows where to strike.

DIANE DE POITIERS

I don't have a warm personal enemy left. They've all died off. I miss them terribly because they helped define me.

CLARE BOOTHE LUCE

Enemies to me are the *sauce piquante* to my dish of life.

ELSA MAXWELL

I will make you shorter by the head.

ELIZABETH I 63

Miss Faithful's press for the employment of ladies, 1862

England _____

The good manners of educated Englishmen . . . Such leaping to feet, such opening of doors, such lightning flourishes with matches and cigarettes—it's all so heroic, I never quite get over the feeling that someone has just said, "To the lifeboats!"

MARGARET HALSEY

Englishwomen's shoes look as if they had been made by someone who had often heard shoes described but who had never seen any.

MARGARET HALSEY

I did a picture in England one winter and it was so cold I almost got married.

SHELLEY WINTERS

Perhaps this country needs an Iron Lady.

MARGARET THATCHER

Fame _____

I've been in *Who's Who* and I know what's what, but it's the first time I ever made the dictionary.

MAE WEST
(on a life jacket being named for her) 65

I stopped believing in Santa Claus when I was six. Mother took me to see him in a department store and he asked for my autograph.

SHIRLEY TEMPLE

The easiest kind of relationship for me is with ten thousand people. The hardest is with one.

JOAN BAEZ

If I'm such a legend, then why am I so lonely? If I'm such a legend, then why do I sit at home for hours staring at the damned telephone, hoping it's out of order, even calling the operator asking her if she's *sure* it's not out of order? Let me tell you, legends are all very well if you've got somebody around who loves you, some man who's not afraid to be in love with Judy Garland.

JUDY GARLAND

Being a sex symbol is a heavy load to carry, especially when one is tired, hurt and bewildered.

CLARA BOW

A sex symbol becomes a thing. I hate being a thing.

MARILYN MONROE

Every man I've ever known has fallen in love with Gilda and wakened with me.

RITA HAYWORTH

I wish I had as much in bed as I get in the newspapers.

LINDA RONSTADT

A friend recently said, "Just imagine *not* being famous—what would happen?" And all of a sudden I saw the face of a passer by on the street and the oddest feeling came over me.

GLORIA SWANSON

The Family ────────────

There is probably nothing like living together for blinding people to each other.

IVY COMPTON-BURNETT

They are not royal. They just happen to have me as their aunt.

QUEEN ELIZABETH II
(about Princess Margaret's children)

I'd like to do a love scene with him just to see what all the yelling is about.

SHIRLEY MACLAINE
(about her brother, Warren Beatty)

Parenthood; that state of being better chaperoned than you were before marriage.

MARCELENE COX

... in times of great stress, such as a four-day vacation, the thin veneer of family life wears off almost at once, and we are revealed in our true personalities.

SHIRLEY JACKSON

She's descended from a long line her mother listened to.

GYPSY ROSE LEE

It takes a woman twenty years to make a man of her son, and another woman twenty minutes to make a fool of him.

HELEN ROWLAND

If it were natural for fathers to care for their sons, they would not need so many laws commanding them to do so.

PHYLLIS CHESLER

A man finds out what is meant by a spitting image when he tries to feed cereal to his infant.

IMOGENE FEY 69

How sad that men would base an entire civilization on the principle of paternity, upon legal ownership and presumed responsibility for children, and then never really get to know their sons and daughters very well.

PHYLLIS CHESLER

The kind of man who thinks that helping with the dishes is beneath him will also think that helping with the baby is beneath him, and then he certainly is not going to be a very successful father.

ELEANOR ROOSEVELT

No man is responsible for his father. That is entirely his mother's affair.

MARGARET TURNBULL

It's shattering to be told your father stinks.

JULIE NIXON

Father's birthday. He would have been 96, 96, yes, today; and could have been 96, like other people one has known: but mercifully was not. His life would have utterly ended mine.

VIRGINIA WOOLF

Fashion ──────────────

Don't ask me what to wear

I have no embroidered
headband from Sardis to
give you, Cleis, such as
I wore
        and my mother
always said that in her
day a purple ribbon
looped in the hair was thought
to be high style indeed

SAPPHO

Oh, yes, I like clothes—on other people. Well, somehow they seem to suffer a sea-change when they get on me. They look quite promising in the shop; and not entirely without hope when I get them back into my wardrobe. But then, when I put them on they tend to deteriorate with a very strange rapidity and one feels so sorry for them.

JOYCE GRENFELL 71

Boots and shoes are the greatest trouble of my life. Everything else one can turn and turn about, and make old look like new; but there's no coaxing boots and shoes to look better than they are.

GEORGE ELIOT

That nonchalant attempt of Eve's
    To fashion garments out of leaves
Was not, as you have heard, inspired
    By shame at being unattired.

MRS. HARRY ST. CLAIR ZOGBAUM

Brevity is the soul of lingerie.

DOROTHY PARKER

It is difficult to see why lace should be so expensive; it is mostly holes.

MARY WILSON LITTLE

We can lie in the language of dress, or try to tell the truth; but unless we are naked and bald, it is impossible to be silent.

ALISON LURIE

Fashion is architecture: it is a matter of proportions.

COCO CHANEL

Glamour is what makes a man ask for your telephone number.
But it is also what makes a woman ask for the name of your
dressmaker.

LILY DACHÉ

My grandfather, Frank Lloyd Wright, wore a red sash on his wedding night. *That* is glamour.

ANNE BAXTER

Don't ever wear artistic jewellery; it wrecks a woman's reputation.

COLETTE

Elegance does not consist in putting on a new dress.

COCO CHANEL

Why not be oneself? That is the whole secret of a successful appearance. If one is a greyhound, why try to look like a Pekingese?

DAME EDITH SITWELL

I base most of my fashion taste on what doesn't itch.

GILDA RADNER

I haven't got the figure for jeans.

MARGARET THATCHER

I tend to wear outfits that match the walls.

DEBRA WINGER

I dress for women, and undress for men.

ANGIE DICKINSON

My weakness is wearing too much leopard print.

JACKIE COLLINS

You'd be surprised how much it costs to look this cheap.

DOLLY PARTON

I always wear slacks because of the brambles and maybe the snakes. And see this basket? I keep everything in it. So I look ghastly, do I? I don't care—so long as I'm comfortable.

KATHARINE HEPBURN

There is nothing new except what is forgotten.

MADEMOISELLE BERTIN
(milliner to Marie Antoinette) 75

Fate

When fate's got it in for you there's no limit to what you may have to put up with.

GEORGETTE HEYER

Do you know how helpless you feel if you have a full cup of coffee in your hand and you start to sneeze?

JEAN KERR

We are no more free agents than the queen of clubs when she takes the knave of hearts.

LADY MARY WORTLEY MONTAGU

It's odd to think we might have been
Sun, moon and stars unto each other—
Only, I turned down one little street
As you went up another.

FANNY HEASLIP LEA

Fortune does not change men; it unmasks them.

SUZANNE NECKER

There is glory in a great mistake.

NATHALIA CRANE

For precocity some great price is always demanded sooner or later in life.

MARGARET FULLER

Martyrdom does not end something, it is only a beginning.

INDIRA GANDHI

Life is something that happens to you while you're making other plans.

MARGARET MILLAR

Food

Before I was born my mother was in great agony of spirit and in a tragic situation. She could take no food except iced oysters and champagne. If people ask me when I began to dance, I reply, "In my mother's womb, probably as a result of the oysters and champagne—the food of Aphrodite."

ISADORA DUNCAN

If I can't have too many truffles I'll do without.

COLETTE

Cooking is like love. It should be entered into with abandon or not at all.

HARRIET VAN HORNE

What I love about cooking is that after a hard day, there is something comforting about the fact that if you melt butter and add flour and then hot stock, IT WILL GET THICK! It's a sure thing! It's a sure thing in a world where nothing is sure.

NORA EPHRON

And now with some pleasure I find that it's seven; and must cook dinner. Haddock and sausage meat. I think it is true that one gains a certain hold on sausage and haddock by writing them down.

VIRGINIA WOOLF

Everything you see I owe to spaghetti.

SOPHIA LOREN 79

Isn't there any other part of the matzo you can eat?

MARILYN MONROE
(when served matzo ball soup three times in a row)

Large, naked, raw carrots are acceptable as food only to those who live in hutches eagerly awaiting Easter.

FRAN LEBOWITZ

. . . nobody really likes capers no matter what you do with them. Some people *pretend* to like capers, but the truth is that any dish that tastes good with capers in it, tastes even better with capers not in it.

NORA EPHRON

Life is too short to stuff a mushroom.

SHIRLEY CONRAN

Summer has an unfortunate effect upon hostesses who have been unduly influenced by the photography of Irving Penn and take the season as a cue to serve dinners of astonishingly meager proportions. These they call light, a quality which, while most assuredly welcome in comedies, cotton shirts and hearts, is not an appropriate touch at dinner.

FRAN LEBOWITZ

It's so beautifully arranged on the plate—you know someone's fingers have been all over it.

JULIA CHILD
(on nouvelle cuisine)

Let them eat cake.

MARIE ANTOINETTE

Friendship _____

Friendships begin with liking or gratitude—roots that can be pulled up.

GEORGE ELIOT

Friendship is the finest balm for the pangs of despised love.

JANE AUSTEN 81

A woman wants her friend to be perfect. She sets a pattern, usually a reasonable facsimile of herself, lays a friend out on this pattern and worries and prods at any little qualities which do not coincide with her own image.

BETTY MACDONALD

Friendship is not possible between two women one of whom is very well dressed.

LAURIE COLWIN

I have lost friends, some by death . . . others by sheer inability to cross the street.

VIRGINIA WOOLF

For of all the hard things to bear and grin,
The hardest is being taken in.

PHOEBE CARY

She's my best friend. I hate her.

RICHMAL CROMPTON

Gossip

For what do we live, but to make sport for our neighbors, and laugh at them in our turn?

JANE AUSTEN

If you haven't got anything nice to say about anybody, come sit next to me.

ALICE ROOSEVELT LONGWORTH

Nobody's interested in sweetness and light.

HEDDA HOPPER

Show me someone who never gossips and I'll show you someone who isn't interested in people.

BARBARA WALTERS

Human nature is so well disposed toward those in interesting situations, that a young person who either marries or dies, is sure to be kindly spoken of.

JANE AUSTEN

People do gossip

And they say about
Leda, that she

once found an egg
hidden under

wild hyacinths.

SAPPHO

Grief

Sorrow is so easy to express and yet so hard to tell.

JONI MITCHELL

You needn't be trying to comfort me—I tell you my
  dolly is dead!
There's no use in saying she isn't, with a crack like
  that in her head.

MARGARET VANDERGRIFT

Grief is so selfish.

MARY ELIZABETH BRADDON

Happiness ────────

If only we'd stop trying to be happy we'd have a pretty good time.

EDITH WHARTON

Happiness is good health and a bad memory.

INGRID BERGMAN

To be happy, one must rid oneself of prejudice, be virtuous, healthy, have a capacity for enjoyment and for passion and the ability to lend oneself to illusion . . . Like passion, illusion is not something you can have if it is not in your nature. However, you can avoid looking behind the scenes.

MADAME DU CHÂTELET

The happiest women, like the happiest nations, have no history.

GEORGE ELIOT

The universal demand for happiness and the widespread un-happiness in our society (and these are but two sides of the same coin) are among the most persuasive signs that we have begun to live in a labor society which lacks enough laboring to keep it contented, for only the *animal laborans,* and neither the craftsman nor the man of action, has ever demanded to be "happy" or thought that mortal man could be happy.

HANNAH ARENDT

Talk happiness. The world is sad enough
Without your woe. No path is wholly rough.

ELLA WHEELER WILCOX

History

Real solemn history, I cannot be interested in . . . The quarrels of popes and kings, with wars or pestilences in every page; the men all so good for nothing, and hardly any women at all.

JANE AUSTEN

88 *Deborah Simpson, acting as courier, presents a letter to General Washington*

Every major horror of history was committed in the name of an altruistic motive. Has any act of selfishness ever equalled the carnage perpetuated by disciples of altruism?

AYN RAND

Revolutionaries do not make revolutions. The revolutionaries are those who know when power is lying in the street and then they can pick it up.

HANNAH ARENDT

Oppressed people are frequently very oppressive when first liberated . . . They know best two positions. Somebody's foot on their neck or their foot on somebody's neck.

FLORYNCE KENNEDY

When the freedom they wished for most was freedom from responsibility, then Athens ceased to be free and was never free again.

EDITH HAMILTON

"How wonderful it must have been for the Ancient Britons," my mother said once, "when the Romans arrived and they could have a Hot Bath."

KATHARINE WHITEHORN 89

After us the deluge.

MADAME DE POMPADOUR

[Napoleon] Bonaparte is nothing more than a Robespierre on horseback.

MADAME DE STAËL

When [Queen Victoria] went to stay at Balmoral in her latter years a number of privies were caused to be built at the backs of the little cottages which had not previously possessed privies. This was to enable the Queen to go on her morning drive round the countryside in comfort, and to descend from her carriage from time to time, ostensibly to visit the humble cottagers in their dwellings. Eventually, word went round that Queen Victoria was exceedingly democratic. Of course it was all due to her little weakness. But everyone copied the Queen and the idea spread, and now you see we have a great democracy.

MURIEL SPARK

They accuse Rasputin of kissing women, etc. Read the Apostles; they kissed everybody as a form of greeting.

CZARINA ALEXANDRA
(in a letter to the Czar)

I met Eva [Peron] in South America when she was nothing but a little cantina girl . . . She was quite attractive and street-smart—she had a Clara Bow look about her. You know, all through history the rogues are the ones who live forever in people's minds and imaginations. Eventually they'll do a musical on Imelda Marcos, the way they did on Evita.

LINA BASQUETTE

Homosexuality ———

Girls who put out are tramps. Girls who don't are ladies. This is, however, a rather archaic usage of the word. Should one of you boys happen upon a girl who doesn't put out, do not jump to the conclusion that you have found a lady. What you have probably found is a Lesbian.

FRAN LEBOWITZ

Once you know what women are like, men get kind of boring. I'm not trying to put them down, I mean I like them sometimes as people, but sexually they're dull.

RITA MAE BROWN 91

If homosexuality were the normal way God would have made Adam and Bruce.

ANITA BRYANT

If boys are better, why should a male choose to love an inferior female? If a penis is so great, two penises should be even greater. In large and small ways, boys are actually conditioned against heterosexuality because society is so relentlessly "for" masculinity.

LETTY COTTIN POGREBIN

Men are weak and constantly need reassurance, so now that they fail to find adulation in the opposite sex, they're turning to each other. Less and less do men need women. More and more do gentlemen prefer gentlemen.

ANITA LOOS

The middle-age of buggers is not to be contemplated without horror.

VIRGINIA WOOLF

Housework _____

The sentimental cult of domestic virtues is the cheapest method at society's disposal of keeping women quiet without seriously considering their grievances or improving their position.

ALVA MYRDAL and VIOLA KLEIN

I hate housework! You make the beds, you do the dishes— and six months later you have to start all over again.

JOAN RIVERS

People invite me to dinner not because I cook, but because I like to clean up. I get immediate gratification from Windex. Yes, I do windows.

CAROL BURNETT

Men cook more, and we all know why. It is the only interesting household task. Getting down and scrubbing the floor is done by women, or by the women they've hired.

NORA EPHRON

I prefer the word "homemaker" because "housewife" always implies that there may be a wife someplace else.

BELLA ABZUG

Cleaning your house while your kids are still growing is like shoveling the walk before it stops snowing.

PHYLLIS DILLER

Humility

Humility is not my forte, and whenever I dwell for any length of time on my own shortcomings, they gradually begin to seem mild, harmless, rather engaging little things, not at all like the staring defects in other people's characters.

MARGARET HALSEY 95

Only the untalented can afford to be humble.

SYLVIA MILES

I'm nobody! Who are you?
Are you nobody, too?

EMILY DICKINSON

If I could I would always work in silence and obscurity, and let my efforts be known by their results.

EMILY BRONTË

I am no lover of pompous title, but only desire that my name be recorded in a line or two, which shall briefly express my name, my virginity, the years of my reign, the reformation of religion under it, and my preservation of peace.

ELIZABETH I

Don't be humble. You're not that great.

GOLDA MEIR

Husbands _____

A man is *so* in the way in the house.

MRS. GASKELL 97

It is ridiculous to think you can spend your entire life with just one person. Three is about the right number. Yes, I imagine three husbands would do it.

CLARE BOOTHE LUCE

I think every woman is entitled to a middle husband she can forget.

ADELA ROGERS ST. JOHN

A husband is what is left of the lover after the nerve is extracted.

HELEN ROWLAND

A man in love is incomplete until he is married. Then he is finished.

ZSA ZSA GABOR

Husbands are like fires. They go out if unattended.

ZSA ZSA GABOR

. . . a woman should never use her husband as her confessor; it demands more virtue of him than his situation allows.

GEORGE SAND

You can't change a man, no-ways. By the time his Mummy turns him loose and he takes up with some innocent woman and marries her, he's what he is.

MARJORIE KINNAN RAWLINGS

Why does a woman work ten years to change a man's habits and then complain that he's not the man she married?

BARBRA STREISAND

I have yet to hear a man ask for advice on how to combine marriage and a career.

GLORIA STEINEM

An archaeologist is the best husband a woman can have; the older she gets, the more interested he is in her.

AGATHA CHRISTIE

He was born to be a salesman. He would be an admirable representative of Rolls-Royce. But an ex-King cannot start selling motor-cars.

THE DUCHESS OF WINDSOR
(referring to her husband) 99

There is so little difference between husbands you might as well keep the first.

ADELA ROGERS ST. JOHN

I wasn't allowed to speak while my husband was alive, and since he's gone no one has been able to shut me up.

HEDDA HOPPER

The true male never yet walked
Who liked to listen when his mate talked.

ANNA WICKHAM

I married him for better or worse, but not for lunch.

HAZEL WEISS

The only really masterful noise a man ever makes in a house is the noise of his key, when he is still on the landing, fumbling for the lock.

COLETTE

A man's home may seem to be his castle on the outside; inside, it is more often his nursery.

CLARE BOOTHE LUCE

A man in the house is worth two in the street.

MAE WEST

Infatuation _____

It seems that it is madder never to abandon one's self than often to be infatuated; better to be wounded, a captive and a slave, than always to walk in armour.

MARGARET FULLER

Great passions don't exist—they are liar's fantasies. What do exist are little loves that may last for a short or longer while.

ANNA MAGNANI 101

I am over-run, jungled in my bed, I am infested with a me-
nagerie of desires; my heart is eaten by a dove, a cat scrambles
in the cave of my sex, hounds in my head obey a whipmaster
who cries nothing but havoc as the hours test my endurance
with an accumulation of tortures.

ELIZABETH SMART

Day and night I find neither rest nor peace. If I sleep I am
disturbed by tormenting dreams in which I see you, always
severe, always grave, always incensed against me. Forgive me
then, Monsieur, if I adopt the course of writing to you again.
How can I endure life if I make no effort to ease its suffer-
ings . . .

CHARLOTTE BRONTË
(letter to her Belgian professor)

I have drunk the wine of life at last, I have known the best
thing best worth knowing, I have been warmed through and
through, never to grow quite cold again till the end.

EDITH WHARTON
(on falling in love for the first time at age forty-six)

Every young girl . . . tries to smother her first love in possessiveness. Oh what tears and rejection await the girl who imbues her first delicate match with fantasies of permanence, expecting that he at this gelatinous stage will fit with her in a finished puzzle for all the days.

GAIL SHEEHY

For though I know he loves me
Tonight my heart is sad
His kiss was not so wonderful
As all the dreams I had.

SARA TEASDALE

At seventeen, you tend to go in for unhappy love affairs.

FRANÇOISE SAGAN

Next to being married, a girl likes to be crossed in love, a little now and then.

JANE AUSTEN

I did not sleep. I never do when I am over-happy, over-unhappy, or in bed with a strange man.

EDNA O'BRIEN 103

Of her scorn the maid repented,
And the shepherd—of his love.

ANNE LETITIA BARBAULD

Loneliness is never more cruel than when it is felt in close propinquity with someone who has ceased to communicate.

GERMAINE GREER

Infatuation means, "A love that it is inconvenient to go on with."

CELIA FREMLIN

I don't remember any love affairs. One must keep love affairs quiet.

THE DUCHESS OF WINDSOR

Where are the loves that we have loved before
When once we are alone, and shut the door?

WILLA CATHER

Infidelity _____

I don't think there are any men who are faithful to their wives.

JACQUELINE KENNEDY ONASSIS

I have always held that it was a very good thing for a young girl to fall hopelessly in love with a married man so that, later on and in the opposite predicament, she could remember what an unassailable citadel a marriage can be.

KATHARINE WHITEHORN

The world wants to be cheated. So cheat.

XAVIERA HOLLANDER

One man's folly is another man's wife.

HELEN ROWLAND 105

Vows! dost think the gods regard the vows of lovers? They are things made in necessity and ought not to be kept, nor punished when broken.

APHRA BEHN

Husbands are chiefly good lovers when they are betraying their wives.

MARILYN MONROE

People who fight fire with fire usually end up with ashes.

ABIGAIL VAN BUREN

There's nothing like a good dose of another woman to make a man appreciate his wife.

CLARE BOOTHE LUCE

It is better to be unfaithful than to be faithful without wanting to be.

BRIGITTE BARDOT

Adultery is a meanness and a stealing, a taking away from someone what should be theirs, a great selfishness, and surrounded and guarded by lies lest it should be found out. And out of the meanness and selfishness and lying flow love and joy and peace beyond anything that can be imagined.

DAME ROSE MACAULEY

Injustice ─────────────

A hurtful act is the transference to others of the degradation which we bear in ourselves.

SIMONE WEIL

Whipping and abuse are like laudanum; you have to double the dose as the sensibilities decline.

HARRIET BEECHER STOWE

There are different kinds of wrong. The people sinned against are not always the best.

IVY COMPTON-BURNETT

The golf links lie so near the mill
That almost every day
The laboring children can look out
And watch the men at play.

SARAH NORCLIFFE CLEGHORN

When one has been threatened with a great injustice, one accepts a smaller as a favour.

JANE CARLYLE

Ireland _____

When anyone asks me about the Irish character, I say look at the trees. Maimed, stark and misshapen, but ferociously tenacious. The Irish have got gab but are too touchy to be humorous. Me too.

EDNA O'BRIEN

. . . Better still, I could be an Irish man—then I would have all the privileges of being male without giving up the right to be wayward, temperamental and an appealing minority.

KATHARINE WHITEHORN 109

In some parts of Ireland the sleep which knows no waking is always followed by a wake which knows no sleeping.

MARY WILSON LITTLE

Jealousy ───────────────

Man is jealous because of his *amour propre;* woman is jealous because of her lack of it.

GERMAINE GREER

Jealousy is not at all low, but it catches us humbled and bowed down, at first sight.

COLETTE

Anxiety is love's greatest killer. It makes one feel as you might when a drowning man holds onto you. You want to save him, but you know he will strangle you with his panic.

ANAÏS NIN

Jealousy is the fear of losing the thing you love most. It's very normal. Suspicion is the thing that's abnormal.

JERRY HALL

Jealousy is no more than feeling alone against smiling enemies.

ELIZABETH BOWEN

Justice ─────────────────

I find the public passion for justice quite boring and artificial, for neither life nor nature cares if justice is ever done or not.

PATRICIA HIGHSMITH

If we were in Scotland, we could bring it in Not Proven. That's Not Guilty, but don't do it again.

WINIFRED DUKE 111

112 *Women in the 1905 Russian revolution*

A lawsuit is to ordinary life what war is to peacetime. In a lawsuit, everybody on the other side is bad. A trial transcript is a discourse in malevolence.

JANET MALCOLM

Nobody outside of a baby carriage or a judge's chamber believes in an unprejudiced point of view.

LILLIAN HELLMAN

Ladies

I have bursts of being a lady, but it doesn't last long.

SHELLEY WINTERS

I'm no model lady. A model's just an imitation of the real thing.

MAE WEST 113

The word LADY: Most Often Used to Describe Someone You Wouldn't Want to Talk to for Even Five Minutes.

FRAN LEBOWITZ

Every Other Inch A Lady

BEATRICE LILLIE
(title of autobiography)

A lady is one who never shows her underwear unintentionally.

LILLIAN DAY

Good women are no fun. The only good woman I can recall in history was Betsy Ross. And all she ever made was a flag.

MAE WEST

Laughter

He laughs best who laughs last,
The wiseacres vow;
But I am impatient,
I want to laugh now.

CAROLYN WELLS

He who laughs, lasts.

MARY PETTIBONE POOLE 115

It's hard to be funny when you have to be clean.

MAE WEST

A difference of taste in jokes is a great strain on the affections.

GEORGE ELIOT

Laugh and the world laughs with you;
Weep, and you weep alone;
For the sad old earth must borrow its mirth,
But has trouble enough of its own.

ELLA WHEELER WILCOX

Lies

Lying increases the creative faculties, expands the ego, lessens
116 the friction of social contacts . . . it is only in lies, wholeheart-

edly and bravely told, that human nature attains through words and speech the forbearance, the nobility, the romance, the idealism, that—being what it is—it falls so short of in fact and in deed.

CLARE BOOTHE LUCE

I never know how much of what I say is true.

BETTE MIDLER

The woman whose behavior indicates that she will make a scene if she is told the truth asks to be deceived.

ELIZABETH JENKINS

Women love the lie that saves their pride, but never the unflattering truth.

GERTRUDE FRANKLIN ATHERTON

When a man brings his wife flowers for no reason—there's a reason.

MOLLY MCGEE

Calumny is like counterfeit money: many people who would not coin it circulate it without qualms.

DIANE DE POITIERS

I was brought up in a clergyman's household so I am a first-class liar.

DAME SYBIL THORNDIKE

I don't care what is written about me so long as it isn't true.

KATHARINE HEPBURN

Life

The poor wish to be rich, the rich wish to be happy, the single wish to be married, and the married wish to be dead.

ANN LANDERS

Nothing is so good as it seems beforehand.

GEORGE ELIOT

> A young Apollo, golden-haired,
> Stands dreaming on the verge of strife,
> Magnificently unprepared
> For the long littleness of life.

FRANCES CROFTS CORNFORD

There are only two or three human stories, and they go on repeating themselves as fiercely as if they had never happened before.

WILLA CATHER

Experience: A comb life gives you after you lose your hair.

JUDITH STERN

The only thing I regret about my life is the length of it. If I had to live my life again I'd make all the same mistakes—only sooner.

TALLULAH BANKHEAD

Men who pass most comfortably through this world are those who possess good digestions and hard hearts.

HARRIET MARTINEAU

One learns in life to keep silent and draw one's own confusions.

CORNELIA OTIS SKINNER

We're all in this alone.

LILY TOMLIN

Life's what's important. Walking, houses, family. Birth and pain and joy. Acting's just waiting for a custard pie. That's all.

KATHARINE HEPBURN

Nothing seems so tragic to one who is old as the death of one who is young, and this alone proves that life is a good thing.

ZOË AKINS

Literature _____

Books succeed,
And lives fail.

ELIZABETH BARRETT BROWNING

Imaginary evil is romantic and varied; real evil is gloomy, monotonous, barren, boring. Imaginary good is boring; real good is always new, marvelous, intoxicating. "Imaginative literature," therefore, is either boring or immoral or a mixture of both.

SIMONE WEIL 121

Nothing induces me to read a novel except when I have to make money by writing about it. I detest them.

VIRGINIA WOOLF

Stories ought to judge and interpret the world.

CYNTHIA OZICK

Some say life is the thing, but I prefer reading.

RUTH RENDELL

The books we think we ought to read are poky, dull and dry;
The books that we would like to read we are ashamed
to buy;
The books that people talk about we never can recall;
And the books that people give us, Oh, they're the worst
of all.

CAROLYN WELLS

I was never allowed to read the popular American children's books of my day because, as my mother said, the children spoke bad English *without the author's knowing it.*

EDITH WHARTON

If I read a book that impresses me, I have to take myself firmly in hand before I mix with other people; otherwise they would think my mind rather queer.

ANNE FRANK

The one thing I regret is that I will never have time to read all the books I want to read.

FRANÇOISE SAGAN

"And what are you reading, Miss ———?" "Oh, it is only a novel!" replies the young lady: while she lays down her book with affected indifference, or momentary shame.—"It is only Cecilia, or Camilla, or Belinda:" or, in short, only some work in which the most thorough knowledge of human nature, the happiest delineation of its varieties, the liveliest effusions of wit and humor are conveyed to the world in the best chosen language.

JANE AUSTEN

I have discovered that our great favourite, Miss Austen, is my country-woman . . . with whom mamma before her marriage was acquainted. Mamma says that she was then the prettiest, silliest, most affected, husband-hunting butterfly she ever remembers.

MARY RUSSELL MITFORD 123

Her books are domestic in the sense that Oedipus Rex is domestic. Her moral dilemmas are often drawn in precisely oedipal terms.

BRIGID BROPHY
(on Jane Austen)

Jane Austen was a complete and most sensible lady, but a very incomplete and rather insensible (*not senseless*) woman. If this is heresy, I cannot help it.

CHARLOTTE BRONTË

Walter Scott has no business to write novels, especially good ones. It is not fair—He has Fame and Profit enough as a Poet, and should not be taking the bread out of other people's mouths. I do not like him, & do not mean to like Waverley if I can help it—but fear I must.

JANE AUSTEN

I am reading Henry James . . . and feel myself as one entombed in a block of smooth amber.

VIRGINIA WOOLF

Henry James chews more than he bites off.

MRS. HENRY ADAMS

Why don't you write books people can read?

NORA JOYCE
(to her husband, James)

The work of a queasy undergraduate scratching his pimples.

VIRGINIA WOOLF
(on Joyce's Ulysses)

Having been unpopular in high school is not just cause for book publication.

FRAN LEBOWITZ

Philip Roth is a good writer, but I wouldn't want to shake hands with him.

JACQUELINE SUSANN

Perversity is the muse of modern literature.

SUSAN SONTAG

The mystery's very much the modern morality play. You have an almost ritual killing and a victim, you have a murderer who in some sense represents the forces of evil, you have your 125 detective coming in—very likely to avenge the death—who represents justice, retribution. And in the end you restore order out of disorder.

P. D. JAMES

The thriller is the cardinal twentieth-century form. All it, like the twentieth century, wants to know is: Who's Guilty?

BRIGID BROPHY

Everywhere I go I'm asked if I think the university stifles writers. My opinion is that they don't stifle enough of them. There's many a bestseller that could have been prevented by a good teacher.

FLANNERY O'CONNOR

We romantic writers are there to make people feel and not think. A historical romance is the only kind of book where chastity really counts.

BARBARA CARTLAND

As artists they're rot, but as providers they're oil wells—they gush.

DOROTHY PARKER
(on lady novelists)

I have the conviction that excessive literary production is a social offense.

GEORGE ELIOT

Honoré Daumier, The Bluestocking Series: The Literary Club

Love

I am so convinced that love is a nuisance, that I am delighted my friends and I are exempt.

MADAME DE LA FAYETTE
(at twenty)

If it is your time love will track you down like a cruise missile. If you say "No! I don't want it right now," that's when you'll get it for sure. Love will make a way out of no way. Love is an exploding cigar which we willingly smoke.

LYNDA BARRY

To fall in love you have to be in the state of mind for it to take, like a disease.

NANCY MITFORD

Love's a disease. But curable . . . Did you ever look through a microscope at a drop of pond water? You see plenty of love there. All the amoebae getting married. I presume they think it very exciting and important. We don't.

DAME ROSE MACAULEY

Every little girl knows about love. It is only her capacity to suffer because of it that increases.

FRANÇOISE SAGAN

Love is the history of a woman's life; it is an episode in man's.

MADAME DE STAËL

Don't threaten me with love, baby. Let's just go walking in the rain.

BILLIE HOLIDAY

Delicacy is to love what grace is to beauty.

MADAME DE MAINTENON

In love there are two things—bodies and words.

JOYCE CAROL OATES

Love conquers all things except poverty and toothache.

MAE WEST

We cease loving ourselves if no one loves us.

MADAME DE STAËL

One hour of right-down love
Is worth an age of dully living on.

APHRA BEHN

Great loves too must be endured.

COCO CHANEL

Lovers. Not a soft word, as people thought, but cruel and tearing.

ALICE MUNRO

Pride—that's a luxury a woman in love can't afford.

CLARE BOOTHE LUCE

I could follow him around the world in my shift.

MARY, QUEEN OF SCOTS
(of James Hepburn, Earl of Bothwell)

"His love is violent but base": a possible sentence.
"His love is deep but base": an impossible one.

SIMONE WEIL

Many emotions go under the name of love, and almost any
one of them will for a while divert the mind from the real, true,
and perfect thing.

RUTH RENDELL

If thou must love me, let it be for nought
Except for love's sake only. Do not say
"I love her for her smile—her look—her way
Of speaking gently,—for a trick of thought
That falls in well with mine, and certes brought
A sense of pleasant ease on such a day"—
For these things in themselves Beloved, may

131

Be changed or change for thee,—and love, so wrought,
May be unwrought so. Neither love me for
Thine own dear pity's wiping my cheeks dry,—
A creature might forget to weep, who bore
Thy comfort long, and lose thy love thereby!
But love me for love's sake, that evermore
Thou mayest love on, through love's eternity.

ELIZABETH BARRETT BROWNING

Love is purely a creation of the human imagination . . . the
most important example of how the imagination continually
outruns the creature it inhabits.

KATHERINE ANNE PORTER

Love . . . is the extremely difficult realization that something
other than oneself is real.

IRIS MURDOCH

Whoso loves
Believes the impossible.

ELIZABETH BARRETT BROWNING

Love, love, love—all the wretched cant of it, masking egotism, lust, masochism, fantasy under a mythology of sentimental postures, a welter of self-induced miseries and joys, blinding and masking the essential personalities in the frozen gestures of courtship, in the kissing and the dating and the desire, the compliments and the quarrels which vivify its barrenness.

GERMAINE GREER

No one has ever loved anyone the way everyone wants to be loved.

MIGNON McLAUGHLIN

Love: that's self-love *à deux*.

MADAME DE STAËL

Love, in distinction from friendship, is killed, or rather extinguished, the moment it is displayed in public.

HANNAH ARENDT

Love ceases to be a pleasure, when it ceases to be a secret.

APHRA BEHN 133

Love is so much better when you're not married.

MARIA CALLAS

People talk about love as though it were something you could give, like an armful of flowers.

ANNE MORROW LINDBERGH

The more you love someone the more he wants from you and the less you have to give since you've already given him your love.

NIKKI GIOVANNI

Love is not enough. It must be the foundation, the cornerstone, but not the complete structure. It is much too pliable. Too yielding.

BETTE DAVIS

Love doesn't just sit there, like a stone, it has to be made, like bread; remade all the time, made new.

URSULA K. LE GUIN

This is the worst of life, that love does not give us common sense, but is a sure way of losing it. We love people, and we say that we were going to do more for them than friendship, but it makes such fools of us that we do far less, indeed sometimes what we do could be mistaken for the work of hatred.

DAME REBECCA WEST

To love without criticism is to be betrayed.

DJUNA BARNES

To be loved is very demoralizing.

KATHARINE HEPBURN 135

Love never dies of starvation, but often of indigestion.

NINON DE L'ENCLOS

In the arithmetic of love, one plus one equals everything, and two minus one equals nothing.

MIGNON MCLAUGHLIN

I leave before being left. *I* decide.

BRIGITTE BARDOT

A sharp knife cuts the quickest and hurts the least.

KATHARINE HEPBURN

Scratch a lover and find a foe.

DOROTHY PARKER

All discarded lovers should be given a second chance, but with somebody else.

MAE WEST

It's not till sex has died out between a man and a woman that they can really love . . . When I look back on the pain of sex, the love like a wild fox so ready to bite, the antagonism that sits like a twin beside love, and contrast it with affection, so deeply unrepeatable, of two people who have lived a life together (and of whom one must die) it's the affection I find richer. It's that I would have again. Not all those doubtful rainbow colors. (But then she's old, one must say.)

ENID BAGNOLD

Manners ─────────────

In society it is etiquette for ladies to have the best chairs and get handed things. In the home the reverse is the case. This is why ladies are more sociable than gentlemen.

VIRGINIA GRAHAM

The perfect hostess will see to it that the works of male and female authors be properly separated on her bookshelves. Their proximity, unless they happen to be married, should not be tolerated.

LADY GOUGH'S ETIQUETTE
(1836)

I have always thought that there is no more fruitful source of family discontent than badly cooked dinners and untidy ways.

ISABELLA BEETON

The three great stumbling blocks in a girl's education, she says, are *homard à l'Americaine,* a boiled egg, and asparagus. Shoddy table manners, she says, have broken up many a happy home.

COLETTE

A car is useless in New York, essential anywhere else. The same with good manners.

MIGNON McLAUGHLIN

It is possible that blondes also prefer gentlemen.

MAMIE VAN DOREN

He is every other inch a gentleman.

DAME REBECCA WEST

It is a gentleman's first duty to remember in the morning who it was he took to bed with him.

DOROTHY L. SAYERS

Outer space is no place for a person of breeding.

LADY VIOLET BONHAM CARTER 139

Marriage ━━━━━━━━━

Bad enough to make mistakes, without going ahead and marrying them.

CRAIG RICE

Never marry a man who hates his mother because he'll end up hating you.

JILL BENNETT

Don't marry a man to reform him—that's what reform schools are for.

MAE WEST

It isn't tying himself to one woman that a man dreads when he thinks of marrying; it's separating himself from all the others.

HELEN ROWLAND

It is a truth universally acknowledged, that a single man in possession of a good fortune, must be in want of a wife.

JANE AUSTEN

Propinquity does it.

MRS. HUMPHREY WARD

A lady's imagination is very rapid; it jumps from admiration to love, from love to matrimony in a moment.

JANE AUSTEN

"You, poor and obscure, and small and plain as you are—I entreat you to accept me as a husband." (Mr. Rochester proposing in *Jane Eyre*.)

CHARLOTTE BRONTË

An engaged woman is always more agreeable than a disengaged. She is satisfied with herself. Her cares are over, and she feels that she may exert all her powers of pleasing without suspicion.

JANE AUSTEN

We're having a little disagreement. What *I* want is a big church wedding with bridesmaids and flowers and a no-expense-spared reception and what *he* wants is to break off our engagement.

SALLY POPLIN

Reader, I married him.

CHARLOTTE BRONTË

Among all the forms of absurd courage, the courage of girls is outstanding. Otherwise there would be fewer marriages . . .

COLETTE

Marriage is a lottery in which men stake their liberty and women their happiness.

VIRGINIE DES RIEUX

A fool and his money are soon married.

CAROLYN WELLS

Love-matches are made by people who are content, for a month of honey, to condemn themselves to a life of vinegar.

THE COUNTESS OF BLESSINGTON

The people people work with best
    Are sometimes very queer;
The people people own by birth
    Quite shock your first idea.
The people people have for friends
    Your common sense appall
But the people people marry
    Are the queerest folk of all.

CHARLOTTE PERKINS GILMAN

I married beneath me. All women do.

NANCY, LADY ASTOR

I've married a few people I shouldn't have, but haven't we all?

MAMIE VAN DOREN 143

He loved me absolutely, that's why he hates me absolutely.

FRIEDA LAWRENCE
(MRS. D. H.)

It is true that I never should have married, but I didn't want to live without a man. Brought up to respect the conventions, love had to end in marriage. I'm afraid it did.

BETTE DAVIS

The surest way to be alone is to get married.

GLORIA STEINEM

When a girl marries she exchanges the attention of many men for the inattention of one.

HELEN ROWLAND

Marrying a man is like buying something you've been admiring for a long time in a shop window. You may love it when you get it home, but it doesn't always go with everything else in the house.

JEAN KERR

The trouble with some women is that they get all excited about nothing—and then marry him.

CHER

Wedlock: the deep, deep peace of the double bed after the hurly-burly of the *chaise longue*.

MRS. PATRICK CAMPBELL

I know a lot of people didn't expect our relationship to last—but we've just celebrated our two months anniversary.

BRITT EKLAND

In Hollywood all marriages are happy. It's trying to live together afterwards that causes all the problems.

SHELLEY WINTERS

God, for two people to be able to live together for the rest of their lives is almost unnatural.

JANE FONDA

Marriage: A souvenir of love.

HELEN ROWLAND 145

In almost every marriage there is a selfish and an unselfish partner. A pattern is set up and soon becomes inflexible, of one person always making the demands and one person always giving way.

IRIS MURDOCH

Marriage must be a relation either of sympathy or of conquest.

GEORGE ELIOT

Chains do not hold a marriage together. It is threads, hundreds of tiny threads which sew people together through the years. This is what makes a marriage last—more than passion or even sex!

SIMONE SIGNORET

It was a nice day. Hal didn't lose his temper with me once.

DOROTHY THOMPSON
(about her husband, Sinclair Lewis)

Why do you always, when you mention my name in your 146 diaries, speak so ill of me? Why do you want all future gen-

erations and our descendants to hold my name in con-
tempt . . . [are you] afraid that your glory after death will be
diminished unless you show me to have been your torment
and yourself as a martyr, bearing a cross in the form of your
wife?

SONYA TOLSTOY
(in a letter to her husband)

Nobody could sleep with Dick. He wakes up during the night,
switches on the lights, speaks into his tape recorder, or takes
notes—it's impossible.

PAT NIXON

All married couples should learn the art of battle as they should
learn the art of making love. Good battle is objective and
honest—never vicious and cruel. Good battle is healthy and
constructive and brings to a marriage the principle of equal
partnership.

ANN LANDERS

Never go to bed mad. Stay up and fight.

PHYLLIS DILLER 147

One wishes marriage for one's daughters and, for one's descendants, better luck.

FAY WELDON

The Media _____

Everybody gets so much information all day long that they lose their common sense.

GERTRUDE STEIN

You should always believe all you read in the newspapers, as this makes them more interesting.

DAME ROSE MACAULEY

Journalism is the ability to meet the challenge of filling space.

DAME REBECCA WEST

For the very first time the young are seeing history being made before it is censored by their elders.

MARGARET MEAD

Every journalist who is not too stupid or too full of himself to notice what is going on knows that what he does is morally indefensible. He is a kind of confidence man, preying on people's vanity, ignorance, or loneliness, gaining their trust and betraying them without remorse.

JANET MALCOLM

The freedom of the press works in such a way that there is not much freedom from it.

PRINCESS GRACE OF MONACO

I used to get on great with journalists until I married Paul.

LINDA McCARTNEY 149

Men

If the world were a logical place, men would ride side-saddle.

RITA MAE BROWN

If man is only a little lower than the angels, the angels should reform.

MARY WILSON LITTLE

Men are nicotine-soaked, beer-besmirched, whisky-greased, red-eyed devils.

CARRY NATION

There's nineteen men livin' in my neighborhood,
Eighteen of them are fools and the one ain't
no doggone good.

BESSIE SMITH

The male sex, as a sex, does not universally appeal to me. I find the men today less manly; but a woman of my age is not in a position to know exactly how manly they are.

KATHARINE HEPBURN

His mother should have thrown him away and kept the stork.

MAE WEST

A bachelor never quite gets over the idea that he is a thing of beauty and a boy forever.

HELEN ROWLAND

Old men are like that, you know. It makes them feel important to think they're in love with somebody.

WILLA CATHER

Men's men: gentle or simple, they're much of a muchness.

GEORGE ELIOT

Macho does not prove mucho.

ZSA ZSA GABOR

Men who are insecure about their masculinity often challenge me to fights.

HONOR BLACKMAN

I like men to behave like men—strong and childish.

FRANÇOISE SAGAN

Mad, bad, and dangerous to know.

LADY CAROLINE LAMB
(on Byron)

I require only three things of a man. He must be handsome, ruthless, and stupid.

DOROTHY PARKER

I have a big flaw in that I am attracted to thin, tall, good-looking men who have one common denominator. They must be lurking bastards.

EDNA O'BRIEN

No nice men are good at getting taxis.

KATHARINE WHITEHORN

Every man I meet wants to protect me. I can't figure out what from.

MAE WEST

Men are creatures with two legs and eight hands.

JAYNE MANSFIELD

Never trust a husband too far, nor a bachelor too near.

HELEN ROWLAND 153

Let's face it, when an attractive but ALOOF ("cool") man comes along, there are some of us who offer to shine his shoes with our underpants. If he has a mean streak, somehow this is "attractive." There are thousands of scientific concepts as to why this is so, and yes, yes, it's very sick—but none of this helps.

LYNDA BARRY

None of you [men] ask for anything—except everything, but just for so long as you need it.

DORIS LESSING

All men are not slimy warthogs. Some men are silly giraffes, some woebegone puppies, some insecure frogs. But if one is not careful, those slimy warthogs can ruin it for all the others.

CYNTHIA HEIMEL

I refuse to consign the whole male sex to the nursery. I insist on believing that some men are my equals.

BRIGID BROPHY

The male is a domestic animal which, if treated with firmness and kindness, can be trained to do most things.

JILLY COOPER

All the men on my staff can type.

BELLA ABZUG

... beware of men who cry. It's true that men who cry are sensitive to and in touch with feelings, but the only feelings they tend to be sensitive to and in touch with are their own.

NORA EPHRON

Men are always ready to respect anything that bores them.

MARILYN MONROE

Getting along with men isn't what's truly important. The vital knowledge is how to get along with a man. One man.

PHYLLIS McGINLEY

Men, being conditioned badly, are always feeling nooses closing around their necks, even dumpy boors no girl would take on a bet.

CYNTHIA HEIMEL

Most women set out to try to change a man, and when they have changed him they do not like him.

MARLENE DIETRICH

Probably the only place where a man can feel really secure is in a maximum security prison, except for the imminent threat of release.

GERMAINE GREER

No man is a hero to his valet.

MADAME CORNUEL

Mountains appear more lofty the nearer they are approached, but great men resemble them not in this particular.

THE COUNTESS OF BLESSINGTON

I have had my belly full of great men (forgive the expression). I quite like to read about them in the pages of Plutarch, where they don't outrage my humanity. Let us see them carved in marble or cast in bronze, and hear no more about them. In real life they are nasty creatures, persecuters, temperamental, despotic, bitter and suspicious.

GEORGE SAND

All Men would be tyrants if they could . . . That your Sex are Naturally Tyrannical is a Truth so thoroughly established as to admit of no dispute.

ABIGAIL ADAMS
(in a letter to John Adams)

It's a man's world, and you men can have it.

KATHERINE ANNE PORTER 157

Men and Women ──────

Men and women, women and men. It will never work.

ERICA JONG

Man and woman are two locked caskets, of which each contains the key to the other.

ISAK DINESEN

The reason husbands and wives do not understand each other is because they belong to different sexes.

DOROTHY DIX

It is hardly too much to say that most domestic tragedies are caused by the feminine intuition of men and the want of it in women.

ADA LEVERSON

Women are not men's equals in anything except responsibility. We are not their inferiors either, or even their superiors. We are quite simply a different race.

PHYLLIS MCGINLEY

The main difference between men and women is that men are lunatics and women are idiots.

DAME REBECCA WEST

Women speak because they wish to speak, whereas a man speaks only when driven to speech by something outside himself—like, for instance, he can't find any clean socks.

JEAN KERR

Men are generally more law-abiding than women. Women have the feeling that since they didn't make the rules, the rules have nothing to do with them.

DIANE JOHNSON

When men reach their sixties and retire, they go to pieces. Women go right on cooking.

GAIL SHEEHY 159

A woman's a woman until the day she dies, but a man's only a man as long as he can.

MOMS MABLEY

The first time Adam had a chance, he laid the blame on woman.

NANCY, LADY ASTOR

If a person continues to see only giants, it means he is still looking at the world through the eyes of a child. I have a feeling that man's fear of woman comes from having first seen her as the mother, creator of men.

ANAÏS NIN

Whatever women do they must do twice as well as men to be thought half as good.

CHARLOTTE WHITTON

The male has been taught that he is superior to women in nearly every way, and that is reinforced by the submissive 160 tactics of many women in their desperate antics of flirtation and hunting; it would be a wonder if the average male did not come to believe that he was superior.

JOYCE CAROL OATES

Men don't like nobility in woman. Not any men. I suppose it is because the men like to have the copyrights on nobility—if there is going to be anything like that in a relationship.

DOROTHY PARKER

. . . perhaps men should think twice before making widowhood our only path to power.

GLORIA STEINEM

God made men stronger but not necessarily more intelligent. He gave women intuition and femininity. And, used properly, that combination easily jumbles the brain of any man I've ever met.

FARRAH FAWCETT

The average man is more interested in a woman who is interested in him than he is in a woman with beautiful legs.

MARLENE DIETRICH 161

A man who is honest with himself wants a woman to be soft and feminine, careful of what she's saying and talk like a man.

ANN-MARGRET

The success of any man with any woman is apt to displease even his best friends.

MADAME DE STAËL

Why are women so much more interesting to men than men are to women?

VIRGINIA WOOLF

A woman need know but one man well, in order to understand all men; whereas a man may know all women and understand not one of them.

HELEN ROWLAND

Women have served all these centuries as looking glasses possessing the . . . power of reflecting the figure of man at twice its natural size.

VIRGINIA WOOLF

He may be fat, stupid and old, but none the less he can condemn the woman's flabby body and menopause and encounter only sympathy if he exchanges her for a younger one.

LIV ULLMANN

... older woman younger man! Popular wisdom claims that this particular class of love affair is the most poignant, tender, poetic, exquisite one there is, altogether the choicest on the menu.

DORIS LESSING

The real paradox is that the men who make, materially, the biggest sacrifices for their women should do the least for them ideally and romantically.

EDITH WHARTON

The only time a woman really succeeds in changing a man is when he's a baby.

NATALIE WOOD

When a woman behaves like a man, why doesn't she behave like a nice man?

DAME EDITH EVANS 163

It is so many years now since Adam and Eve were first together in the garden, that it seems a great pity that we have not learned better how to please one another . . . I wish that once, in all the time of men and women, two ambassadors could meet in a friendly mind and come to understand each other.

ISAK DINESEN

Women want mediocre men, and men are working hard to become as mediocre as possible.

MARGARET MEAD

There is more difference within the sexes than between them.

IVY COMPTON-BURNETT

Misery ─────────────

It's a long old road, but I'm gonna find the end;
And when I get back I'm gonna shake hands with a friend.

On the side of the road, I sat underneath a tree.
Nobody knows the thought that came over me.

Weepin' and cryin', tears fallin' on the groun',
When I got to the end I was so worried down.

Picked up my bag, baby, and I tried it again.
I got to make it, I've got to find the end.

You can't trust nobody, you might as well be alone,
Found my long lost friend and I might as well stayed at home.

BESSIE SMITH

Ah! I shall repeat it endlessly, the only misfortune is to be
born!

MADAME MARIE DU DEFFAND 165

Those who are unhappy have no need for anything in this world but people capable of giving them their attention.

SIMONE WEIL

Those who do not complain are never pitied.

JANE AUSTEN

God gave a loaf to every bird,
But just a crumb to me.

EMILY DICKINSON

Oh! Why does the wind blow upon me so wild?
Is it because I'm nobody's child?

HENRIETTA CASE

I was, being human, born alone;
I am, being woman, hard beset;
I live by squeezing from a stone
The little nourishment I get.

ELINOR HOYT WYLIE

We are so tired, my heart and I.
Of all things here beneath the sky
Only one thing would please us best—
Endless, unfathomable rest.

MATHILDE BLIND

Oh, God, I'm only twenty and I'll have to go on living and
living and living.

JEAN RHYS
(in her diary)

Money

I've been rich and I've been poor; rich is better.

SOPHIE TUCKER

A single woman with a narrow income must be a ridiculous old maid, the proper sport of boys and girls; but a single woman of good fortune is always respectable, and may be as sensible and pleasant as anybody else.

JANE AUSTEN

The two most beautiful words in the English language are "check enclosed."

DOROTHY PARKER

I never made any money till I took off my pants.

SALLY RAND

Keep cool and collect.

MAE WEST

Money speaks sense in a language all nations understand.

APHRA BEHN

Romance without finance is a nuisance. Few men value free merchandise. Let the chippies fall where they may.

SALLY STANFORD

Algebra and money are essentially levelers; the first intellectually, the second effectively.

SIMONE WEIL

As a cousin of mine once said about money,
money is always there but the pockets change,
it is not in the same pockets after a change,
and that is all there is to say about money.

GERTRUDE STEIN 169

I have known many persons who turned their gold into smoke, but you are the first to turn smoke into gold.

QUEEN ELIZABETH I
(to Sir Walter Raleigh,
on his introduction of tobacco into England)

Hollywood money isn't money. It's congealed snow, melts in your hand, and there you are.

DOROTHY PARKER

I didn't want to be rich, I just wanted enough to get the couch reupholstered.

KATE MOSTEL
(MRS. ZERO MOSTEL)

In the midst of life we are in debt.

ETHEL WATTS MUMFORD

Some couples go over their budgets very carefully every month, others just go over them.

SALLY POPLIN

Why does a slight tax increase cost you two hundred dollars and a substantial tax cut save you thirty cents?

PEG BRACKEN

The richer your friends, the more they will cost you.

ELIZABETH MARBURY

The rich have a passion for bargains as lively as it is pointless.

FRANÇOISE SAGAN

The great rule is not to talk about money with people who have much more or much less than you.

KATHARINE WHITEHORN

No one would remember the Good Samaritan if he only had good intentions. He had money as well.

MARGARET THATCHER

One must be poor to know the luxury of giving.

GEORGE ELIOT

Come away; poverty's catching.

APHRA BEHN

Movies ━━━━━━━━━━━━━━━━

Movies are so rarely great art that if we cannot appreciate the great *trash* we have very little reason to be interested in them.

PAULINE KAEL

I wouldn't say when you've seen one Western you've seen the lot; but when you've seen the lot you get the feeling you've seen one.

KATHARINE WHITEHORN

Science fiction films are not about science; they're about disaster, one of the oldest subjects of art.

SUSAN SONTAG

I think my father ... and the rest of them invented the happy family and put it into movies to drive everyone crazy.

JILL ROBINSON
(about Dore Schary)

I was born at the age of twelve on a Metro-Goldwyn-Mayer lot.

JUDY GARLAND

It's really amazing. I couldn't act. I had that terrible singing voice, and now I can see I wasn't the greatest tap dancer in the world, either.

RUBY KEELER

I used to tremble from nerves so badly that the only way I could hold my head steady was to lower my chin practically to my chest and look up at Bogie. That was the beginning of The Look.

LAUREN BACALL

The relationship between the make-up man and the film actor is that of accomplices in crime.

MARLENE DIETRICH 173

They used to photograph Shirley Temple through gauze. They should photograph me through linoleum.

TALLULAH BANKHEAD

I hate to see myself on the screen. I hate the way I look. I hate the sound of my voice. I'm always thinking I should have played it better.

ELIZABETH TAYLOR

My career started ass-backwards.

RAQUEL WELCH

I believe in censorship. After all, I made a fortune out of it.

MAE WEST

Music ▬▬▬▬▬▬

You ask my opinion about taking the young Salzburg musician [Mozart] into your service. I do not know where you can place him, since I feel that you do not require a composer or other useless people . . . It gives one's service a bad name when such types go about the world like beggars; besides, he has a large family.

MARIA THERESA,
ARCHDUCHESS OF AUSTRIA
(in a letter to her son)

My playing is getting all behindhand, as is always the case when Robert is composing. I cannot find one little hour in the day for myself.

CLARA SCHUMANN

Nobody really sings in an opera—they just make loud noises.

AMELITA GALLI-CURCI 175

An unalterable and unquestioned law of the musical world required that the German text of French operas sung by Swedish artists should be translated into Italian for the clearer understanding of English speaking audiences.

EDITH WHARTON

I can hold a note as long as the Chase National Bank.

ETHEL MERMAN

I wish the Government would put a tax on pianos for the incompetent.

DAME EDITH SITWELL

Your attitude to your audience should be that they're a bunch of non-believers and you're the only person that could convince them.

LINDA RONSTADT

I wish Frank Sinatra would just shut up and sing.

LAUREN BACALL

I know the song and I can make all those noises at home.

QUEEN ELIZABETH II

Rock n' roll is dream soup, what's your brand?

PATTI SMITH

Old Age ───────────────

Cut off my head and I am thirteen.

COCO CHANEL
(on reaching sixty)

Now that I'm over sixty I'm veering toward respectability.

SHELLEY WINTERS

At sixty-three years of age, less a quarter, one still has plans.

COLETTE 177

Old age is like a plane flying through a storm. Once you are aboard there is nothing you can do.

GOLDA MEIR

I used to dread getting older because I thought I would not be able to do all the things I wanted to do, but now that I am older I find that I don't want to do them.

NANCY, LADY ASTOR

As I grow older and older
And totter towards the tomb
I find that I care less and less
Who goes to bed with whom.

DOROTHY L. SAYERS

If you survive long enough, you're revered—rather like an old building.

KATHARINE HEPBURN

I'll be eighty this month. Age, if nothing else, entitles me to set the record straight before I dissolve. I've given my memoirs

far more thought than any of my marriages. You can't divorce
a book.

GLORIA SWANSON

I have a horrible dislike of old age. Everybody's dead—half,
no nearly all of one's contemporaries—and those that aren't
are ga-ga. Someone rang the other day and said, "I want to
invite you and Duff over for dinner." I said, "But Duff's been
dead for twenty-eight years."

LADY DIANA COOPER

... I have reached it [old age] and I should at least like so to arrange matters that I do not travel farther along this path of infirmities, pains, losses of memory and disfigurement. Their attack is at hand, and I hear a voice that says, "You must go along, whatever you may say; or if indeed you will not, then you must die", which is an extremity from which nature recoils. However, that is the fate of all who go on a little too far.

MADAME DE SÉVIGNÉ

Old age is life's parody.

SIMONE DE BEAUVOIR

The years seem to rush by now, and I think of death as a fast approaching end of a journey—double and treble reasons for loving as well as working while it is day.

GEORGE ELIOT

The Penis

A man is two people, himself and his cock. A man always takes his friend to the party. Of the two, the friend is the nicer, being more able to show his feelings.

BERYL BAINBRIDGE

I wonder why men get serious at all. They have this delicate long thing hanging outside their bodies which goes up and down by its own will. If I were a man I would always be laughing at myself.

YOKO ONO

The penis is the only muscle man has that he cannot flex. It is also the only extremity that he cannot control . . . But even worse, as it affects the dignity of its owner, is its seeming obedience to that inferior thing, woman. It rises at the sight, or even at the thought of a woman.

ELIZABETH GOULD DAVIS 181

Freud, of course, was wrong when he claimed that women suffer from penis envy—it is the men who do.

SABRINA SEDGEWICK

People

People on horses look better than they are, people in cars look worse.

MARYA MANNES

Man is a hating rather than a loving animal.

DAME REBECCA WEST

What is man, when you come to think upon him, but a minutely set, ingenious machine for turning, with infinite artfulness, the red wine of Shiraz into urine?

ISAK DINESEN

I've always felt that a person's intelligence is directly reflected by the number of conflicting points of view he can entertain simultaneously on the same topic.

LISA ALTHER

If all the good people were clever,
And all clever people were good,
The world would be nicer than ever
We thought that it possibly could.

But somehow, 'tis seldom or never
The two hit it off as they should;
The good are so harsh to the clever,
The clever so rude to the good!

ELIZABETH WORDSWORTH

One of my correspondents has me convinced that the human race would be saved if the world became one huge nudist colony. I keep thinking how much harder it would be to carry concealed weapons.

CYRA MCFADDEN

The average, healthy, well-adjusted adult gets up at 7:30 in the morning feeling just plain terrible.

JEAN KERR 183

Anything that begins "I don't know how to tell you this," is never good news.

RUTH GORDON

Philosophy ————————————

Steer clear of overviews. Those of us who have the situation in Lebanon in perspective and know exactly how to plot a gay rights campaign are usually morons. We snap at our children when they have innocent homework questions. We don't notice when our lover has a deadline. We forget to call our best friend back when she's just had root canal.

Homework, root canal and deadlines are the important things in life, and only when we have these major dramas taken care of can we presume to look at the larger questions.

CYNTHIA HEIMEL

Philosopher: A man up in a balloon, with his family and friends holding the ropes which confine him to earth and trying to haul him down.

LOUISA MAY ALCOTT

I like trees because they seem more resigned to the way they have to live than other things do.

WILLA CATHER

You have heard me quote from Plato
A thousand times no doubt;
Well, I have discovered that he did not know
What he was talking about.

ELLA WHEELER WILCOX

Bromidic though it may sound, some questions don't have answers, which is a terribly difficult lesson to learn.

KATHARINE GRAHAM

I believe that people would be alive today if there were a death penalty.

NANCY REAGAN

You can never be too rich or too thin.

THE DUCHESS OF WINDSOR

If you want to catch a trout, don't fish in a herring barrel.

ANN LANDERS

General notions are generally wrong.

LADY MARY WORTLEY MONTAGU

Pleasure ⎯⎯⎯⎯⎯⎯⎯⎯

Variety is the soul of pleasure.

APHRA BEHN

One half of the world cannot understand the pleasures of the other.

JANE AUSTEN

To get an idea of our fellow countrymen's miseries, we have only to take a look at their pleasures.

GEORGE ELIOT

Poetry ━━━━━━━━━━━

I hope that one or two immortal lyrics will come out of all this tumbling about.

LOUISE BOGAN
(of her affair with fellow poet Theodore Roethke)

If . . . it makes my whole body so cold no fire can warm me, I know that is poetry.

EMILY DICKINSON

Women's poetry should, above all things, be elegant as a peacock, and there should be a fantastic element, a certain strangeness in its beauty. But above all, let us avoid sentimentality: do not let us write about Pierrot, or Arcady, or how much good we should like to do in the world!

DAME EDITH SITWELL

Poets are the only people to whom love is not only a crucial, 187 but an indispensable experience, which entitles them to mistake it for a universal one.

HANNAH ARENDT

My verses are no damn good.

DOROTHY PARKER

Politics ─────────────

I am firm. You are obstinate. He is a pigheaded fool.

KATHARINE WHITEHORN

Non-violence is a flop. The only bigger flop is violence.

JOAN BAEZ

It is far easier to act under conditions of tyranny than to think.

HANNAH ARENDT

It is better to die on your feet than to live on your knees.

DOLORES IBARRURI
("LA PASIONARIA")

There's never been a good government.

EMMA GOLDMAN

Female vote-catching, 1870

An aristocracy in a republic is like a chicken whose head has been cut off. It may run about in a lovely way, but in fact it's dead.

NANCY MITFORD

Tories are not always wrong, but they are always wrong at the right moment.

LADY VIOLET BONHAM CARTER

Communism is the opiate of the intellectuals.

CLARE BOOTHE LUCE

Ask anyone committed to a Marxist analysis how many angels on the head of a pin, and you will be asked in turn to never mind the angels, tell me who controls the production of pins.

JOAN DIDION

The great mistake of the Marxists and of the whole of the nineteenth century was to think that by walking straight on one mounted upward into the air.

SIMONE WEIL

Ninety-eight percent of the adults in this country are decent, hard-working, honest Americans. It's the other lousy two percent that get all the publicity. But then—we elected them.

LILY TOMLIN

The politicians were talking themselves red, white and blue in the face.

CLARE BOOTHE LUCE

Congress—these, for the most part, illiterate hacks whose fancy vests are spotted with gravy, and whose speeches, hypocritical, unctuous, and slovenly, are spotted along with the gravy of political patronage.

MARY MCCARTHY

One of the things that politics has taught me is that men are not a reasoned or reasonable sex.

MARGARET THATCHER

Never lose your temper with the Press or the public is a major rule of political life.

CHRISTABEL PANKHURST

They say women talk too much. If you have worked in congress you know that the filibuster was invented by men.

CLARE BOOTHE LUCE

In politics, if you want anything said, ask a man; if you want anything done, ask a woman.

MARGARET THATCHER

There is only one political career for which women are perfectly suitable, diplomacy.

CLARE BOOTHE LUCE

The reason there are so few female politicians is that it is too much trouble to put makeup on two faces.

MAUREEN MURPHY

He speaks to me as if I were a public meeting.

QUEEN VICTORIA
(about Gladstone)

If you weren't such a great man you'd be a terrible bore.

MRS. WILLIAM GLADSTONE
(to her husband)

Calvin Coolidge looked as if he had been weaned on a pickle.

ALICE ROOSEVELT LONGWORTH

Thomas E. Dewey is just about the nastiest little man I've ever known. He struts sitting down.

MRS. CLARENCE DYKSTRA

No woman has ever so comforted the distressed—or so distressed the comfortable.

CLARE BOOTHE LUCE
(on Eleanor Roosevelt)

The First Lady is an unpaid public servant elected by one person—her husband.

LADY BIRD JOHNSON 193

I have sacrificed everything in my life that I consider precious in order to advance the political career of my husband.

PAT NIXON

As President Nixon says, presidents can do almost anything, and President Nixon has done many things that nobody would have thought of doing.

GOLDA MEIR

The public is entitled to know whether or not I am married to Jack the Ripper.

GERALDINE FERRARO

Is there life after the White House?

BETTY FORD

Possessions

As soon as our engagement appeared in The Times wedding presents poured in . . . they came in cohorts—fifteen lamps of the same design, forty trays, a hundred and more huge glass vases . . . When the presents were all arranged Lady Evelyn looked at them reflectively.

"The glass will be the easiest," she said. "It only needs a good kick." She said silver was more of a problem. "Walter and I had such luck, *all* ours was stolen while we were on honeymoon."

DIANA MOSLEY 195

I am a marvelous housekeeper. Every time I leave a man I keep his house.

ZSA ZSA GABOR

No gold-digging for me . . . I take diamonds! We may be off the gold standard someday.

MAE WEST

A diamond is the only kind of ice that keeps a girl warm.

ELIZABETH TAYLOR

I never hated a man enough to give him his diamonds back.

ZSA ZSA GABOR

Nothing that costs only a dollar is worth having.

ELIZABETH ARDEN

I don't know how it happens, my car just drives itself to Neiman Marcus.

VICTORIA PRINCIPAL

Diamonds are my service stripes.

MAE WEST

I prefer liberty to chains of diamonds.

LADY MARY WORTLEY MONTAGU

Well! Some people talk of morality, and some of religion but give me a little snug property.

MARIA EDGEWORTH

Prophecy

Prophecy is the most gratuitous form of error.

GEORGE ELIOT

No woman in my time will be Prime Minister or Chancellor or Foreign Secretary—not the top jobs. Anyway I wouldn't want to be Prime Minister. You have to give yourself 100%.

MARGARET THATCHER
(from an interview, 1969)

Psychology

One out of four people in this country is mentally imbalanced. Think of your three closest friends—and if they seem okay, then you're the one.

ANN LANDERS

Freud is the father of psychoanalysis. It has no mother.

GERMAINE GREER

Surely he never wrote his "sexy" books. What a terrible man. I am sure he has never been unfaithful to his wife. It's quite abnormal and scandalous.

ANNA DE NOAILLES
(on meeting Freud)

Psychotherapy, unlike castor oil which will work no matter how you get it down, is useless when forced on an uncooperative patient.

ABIGAIL VAN BUREN

One should only see a psychiatrist out of boredom.

MURIEL SPARK

"You seem to be reacting to your boyfriend as if he were your father," your shrink may say stonily (unless she is a strict Freudian, in which case she'll shut up and wait until you think of it yourself, a process that usually takes ten years. This is why strict Freudians have such lovely summer houses.)

CYNTHIA HEIMEL

There is no such thing as inner peace. There is only nervousness and death.

FRAN LEBOWITZ

Reality is a crutch for people who can't cope with drugs.

LILY TOMLIN

Sanity is a cozy lie.

SUSAN SONTAG

Quotes ━━━━━━━━━━

I might repeat to myself, slowly and soothingly, a list of quotations beautiful from minds profound; if I can remember any of the damn things.

DOROTHY PARKER

If it's a woman, it's caustic; if it's a man, it's authoritative.

BARBARA WALTERS

That's the point of quotations, you know: one can use another's words to be insulting.

AMANDA CROSS

Racial Prejudice —————

Sometimes, it's like a hair across your cheek. You can't see it, you can't find it with your fingers, but you keep brushing at it because the feel of it is irritating.

MARIAN ANDERSON

I knew they were going to make a big deal of my being black, but I wish they'd ask me about my dancing.

VANESSA WILLIAMS 201

You know the phrase "Black is beautiful" was invented by the whites in South Africa to raise the morale of the black people.

MARY FRANCIS
(MRS. DICK FRANCIS)

You can be up to your boobies in white satin, with gardenias in your hair and no sugar cane for miles, but you can still be working on a plantation.

BILLIE HOLIDAY

Religion

I read the book of Job last night—I don't think God comes well out of it.

VIRGINIA WOOLF

Where did your Christ come from? From God and a woman! Man had nothing to do with him.

SOJOURNER TRUTH

Liszt said to me today that God alone deserves to be loved. It may be true, but when one has loved a man it is very different to love God.

GEORGE SAND

Religion converts despair, which destroys, into resignation, which submits.

THE COUNTESS OF BLESSINGTON

Father asked us what was God's noblest work. Anna said *men,* but I said *babies.* Men are often bad; babies never are.

LOUISA MAY ALCOTT
(childhood diary)

The Bible and the Church have been the greatest stumbling blocks in the way of women's emancipation.

ELIZABETH CADY STANTON

Most of my friends are not Christians, but I have some who are Anglicans or Roman Catholics.

DAME ROSE MACAULEY 203

"Place before your eyes two precepts, and only two. One is Preach the Gospel; and the other is—*Put down enthusiasm!*" . . . The church of England in a nutshell.

MRS. HUMPHREY WARD

Giving away a fortune is taking Christianity too far.

CHARLOTTE BINGHAM

A clergyman has nothing to do but to be slovenly and selfish—read the newspaper, watch the weather, and quarrel with his wife. His curate does all the work and the business of his own life is to dine.

JANE AUSTEN

I went to a convent in New York and was fired finally for my insistence that the Immaculate Conception was a spontaneous combustion.

DOROTHY PARKER

Once have a priest for enemy, good bye to peace.

SARAH FLOWER ADAMS

Good for the soul—but bad for the heel.

AGNES GUILFOYLE
(on confession)

204

I always find that statistics are hard to swallow and impossible to digest. The only one I can ever remember is that if all the people who go to sleep in church were laid end to end they would be a lot more comfortable.

MRS. ROBERT A. TAFT

When we talk to God, we're praying. When God talks to us, we're schizophrenic.

LILY TOMLIN

God answers sharp and sudden on some prayers,
And thrusts the thing we have prayed for in our face,
A gauntlet with a gift in't.

ELIZABETH BARRETT BROWNING

Did not God
Sometimes withhold in mercy what we ask,
We should be ruined at our own request.

HANNAH MORE

Millions long for immortality who do not know what to do with themselves on a rainy Sunday afternoon.

SUSAN ERTZ 205

God is love, but get it in writing.

GYPSY ROSE LEE

Romance ————————————

Oh, what a dear ravishing thing is the beginning of an Amour!

APHRA BEHN

Romance is the glamour which turns the dust of everyday life into a golden haze.

ELINOR GLYN

You need someone to love you while you're looking for someone to love.

SHELAGH DELANEY

It is a common enough case, that of a man being suddenly captivated by a woman nearly the opposite of his ideal.

GEORGE ELIOT

A thousand martyrs I have made,
    All sacrific'd to my desire;
A thousand beauties have betray'd,
    That languish in resistless fire.
The untam'd heart to hand I brought,
And fixed the wild and wandering thought.

I never vow'd nor sigh'd in vain
    But both, tho' false, were well receiv'd.
The fair are pleas'd to give us pain,
    And what they wish is soon believ'd.
And tho' I talk'd of wounds and smart,
Love's pleasures only touched my heart.

Alone the glory and the spoil
    I always laughing bore away;
The triumphs, without pain or toil,
    Without the hell, the heav'n of joy.
And while I thus at random rove
Despis'd the fools that whine for love.

APHRA BEHN   207

The head never rules the heart, but just becomes its partner in crime.

MIGNON McLAUGHLIN

And we meet, with champagne and chicken, at last.

LADY MARY WORTLEY MONTAGU

A kiss can be a comma, a question mark or an exclamation point. That's basic spelling that every woman ought to know.

MISTINGUETTE

"Yes," I answered you last night;
"No," this morning, sir, I say.
Colours seen by candlelight
Will not look the same by day.

ELIZABETH BARRETT BROWNING

In a great romance, each person basically plays a part that the other really likes.

ELIZABETH ASHLEY

Man never quite forgets his very first love,
Unless she's true.

MARY KYLE DALLAS

Self-Knowledge ─────

From the age of thirteen I had revelations from our Lord by a voice which told me how to behave.

JOAN OF ARC 209

I am your anointed Queen. I will never be by violence constrained to do anything. I thank God I am endued with such qualities that if I were turned out of the Realm in my petticoat I were able to live in any place in Christome.

ELIZABETH I

Pray, good people, be civil. I am the Protestant whore.

NELL GWYN
(to a hostile crowd that mistook her for the Catholic Duchess of Portland)

I think I may boast myself to be, with all possible vanity, the most unlearned and uninformed female who ever dared to be an authoress.

JANE AUSTEN

I . . . am small, like the wren, and my hair is bold like the chestnut burr; and my eyes like the sherry in the glass that the guest leaves.

EMILY DICKINSON

Since I was twenty-four . . . there never was any vagueness in my plans or ideas as to what God's work was for me.

FLORENCE NIGHTINGALE

No one ever pruned me. If you have been sunned through and through like an apricot on a wall from your earliest days, you are oversensitive to any withdrawal of heat.

MARGOT ASQUITH

What a wonderful life I've had! I only wish I'd realized it sooner.

COLETTE

I never said "I want to be alone." I only said "I want to be let alone."

GRETA GARBO

I invented my life by taking for granted that everything I did not like would have an opposite, which I would like.

COCO CHANEL 211

I succeeded by saying what everyone else is thinking.

JOAN RIVERS

I survived because I was tougher than anybody else.

BETTE DAVIS

I can throw a fit, I'm a master at it.

MADONNA

I hope there's no one else like me.

JANE FONDA

I'm as pure as the driven slush.

TALLULAH BANKHEAD

Deep down I'm pretty superficial.

AVA GARDNER

I always wanted to be some kind of writer or newspaper reporter. But after college . . . I did other things.

JACQUELINE KENNEDY ONASSIS

I'm a tuning fork, tense and twanging all the time.

EDNA O'BRIEN

I am terribly shy, but of course no one believes me. Come to think of it, neither would I.

CAROL CHANNING

I have no regrets. I wouldn't have lived my life the way I did if I was going to worry about what people were going to say.

INGRID BERGMAN

I've been through it all, baby. I'm Mother Courage.

ELIZABETH TAYLOR

First I lost my weight, then I lost my voice, and now I lost Onassis.

MARIA CALLAS

Maybe I'm not talented. Maybe I'm just the Dinah Shore of the 'sixties. The square people think I'm too hip and the hip people think I'm too square. And nobody likes my choice of men—everybody thinks I'm fucking the Mormon Tabernacle Choir.

CHER

When I appear in public people expect me to neigh, grind my teeth, paw the ground and swish my tail—none of which is easy.

PRINCESS ANNE

I'm as thick as a plank.

PRINCESS DIANA

I did not have three thousand pairs of shoes, I had one thousand and sixty.

IMELDA MARCOS

In my long and colorful career, one thing stands out: I have been misunderstood.

MAE WEST

Sex

The zipless fuck was more than a fuck. It was a platonic ideal . . . the zipless fuck is absolutely pure. It is free of ulterior motives. There is no power game. The man is not "taking" and the woman is not "giving." No one is attempting to cuckold a husband or humiliate a wife. No one is trying to prove anything or get anything out of anyone. The zipless fuck is the purest thing there is. And it is rarer than the unicorn.

ERICA JONG 215

Ducking for apples—change one letter and it's the story of my life.

DOROTHY PARKER

She's the original good time that was had by all.

BETTE DAVIS

The girl speaks eighteen languages and can't say no in any of them.

DOROTHY PARKER

It doesn't matter what you do in the bedroom as long as you don't do it in the street and frighten the horses.

MRS. PATRICK CAMPBELL

Is that a gun in your pocket, or are you just glad to see me?

MAE WEST

Whatever else can be said about sex, it cannot be called a dignified performance.

HELEN LAWRENSON

Nature abhors a virgin—a frozen asset.

CLARE BOOTHE LUCE

I shall not say why and how I became, at the age of fifteen, the mistress of the Earl of Craven.

HARRIETTE WILSON
(Memoirs, first sentence)

The light covering of flesh was so transmuted with ecstasy that earthly passion became a heavenly embrace of white, fiery flame.

ISADORA DUNCAN

The requirements of romantic love are difficult to satisfy in the trunk of a Dodge Dart.

LISA ALTHER

To err is human—but it feels divine.

MAE WEST

I'm saving the bass player for Omaha.

JANIS JOPLIN 217

Except for the few years between the invention of The Pill and the discovery of Herpes, sex has always been dangerous.

VOGUE MAGAZINE

Women complain about sex more than men. Their gripes fall into two major categories: (1) Not enough. (2) Too much.

ANN LANDERS

Some men are all right in their place—if they only knew the right places!

MAE WEST

I've tried several varieties of sex. The conventional position makes me claustrophobic. And the others either give me a stiff neck or lockjaw.

TALLULAH BANKHEAD

In real life, women are always trying to mix something up with sex—religion, or babies, or hard cash; it is only men who long for sex separated out, without rings or strings.

KATHARINE WHITEHORN

Unless there's some emotional tie, I'd rather play tennis.

BIANCA JAGGER

The truth is, sex doesn't mean that much to me now.

LANA TURNER

After we made love he took a piece of chalk and made an outline of my body.

JOAN RIVERS

The only reason I would take up jogging is so I could hear heavy breathing again.

ERMA BOMBECK

An orgasm is just a reflex like a sneeze.

DR. RUTH WESTHEIMER

All too many men still seem to believe, in a rather naive and egocentric way, that what feels good to them is automatically what feels good to women.

SHERE HITE

I like a man what takes his time.

MAE WEST 219

I am happy now that Charles calls on my bed chamber less frequently than of old. As it is I now endure but two calls a week and when I hear his steps outside my door I lie down on my bed, close my eyes, open my legs and think of England.

LADY ALICE HILLINGDON
(1912)

The Single Life ─────────

I would not marry God.

MAXINE ELLIOTT
(telegram denying rumors of her marriage)

I can't mate in captivity.

GLORIA STEINEM

Marriage is a great institution, but I'm not ready for an institution.

MAE WEST

There are men I could spend eternity with. But not this life.

KATHLEEN NORRIS

I never married because there was no need. I have three pets at home which answer the same purpose as a husband. I have a dog which growls every morning, a parrot which swears all the afternoon and a cat that comes home late at night.

MARIE CORELLI 221

I would rather be a beggar and single, than a Queen and married . . . I should call the wedding ring the yoke ring.

ELIZABETH I

A woman without a man is like a fish without a bicycle.

GLORIA STEINEM

Being an old maid is like death by drowning, a really delightful sensation after you cease to struggle.

EDNA FERBER

Social Life _____

I do not want people to be agreeable, as it saves me the trouble of liking them.

JANE AUSTEN

Who can begin conventional amiability the first thing in the morning? It is the hour of savage instincts and natural tendencies; it is the triumph of the Disagreeable and the Cross. I am convinced that the Muses and the Graces never thought of having breakfast anywhere but in bed.

COUNTESS VON ARNIM

Some new neighbours, that came a month or two ago, brought with them an accumulation of all the things to be guarded against in a London neighborhood, viz., a pianoforte, a lapdog, and a parrot.

JANE CARLYLE

Being popular is important. Otherwise people might not like you.

MIMI POND

Giving parties is a trivial avocation, but it pays the dues for my union card in humanity.

ELSA MAXWELL

I like high life. I like its manners, its splendors, the beings which move in its enchanted sphere. I like to consider the 223

habits of those beings, their way of thinking, speaking, acting. Let fools talk about the artificial, voluptuous, idle existence spun out by Dukes, Lords, Ladies, Knights and Esquires of high degree. Such cant is not for me.

CHARLOTTE BRONTË

How charming was, and is, the chanciness of being a girl . . . You walk into a drawing-room and a dark man or a light man or a red man may change your life . . . It isn't that

I was what's called, rather unhandsomely, "highly sexed". But it was such a surprise that one could attract. It was like a stream finding out that it could move a rock. The pleasure of one's effect on other people still exists in age—what's called making a hit. But the hit is much rarer and made of different stuff.

ENID BAGNOLD

I don't remember anybody's name. Why do you think the "dahling" thing started?

EVA GABOR

The cocktail party is easily the worst invention since castor oil.

ELSA MAXWELL

It is not done to let anybody be too happy. The moment two people seem to be enjoying one another's company, a good hostess introduces a third element or removes the first.

VIRGINIA GRAHAM

Nothing spoils a good party like a genius.

ELSA MAXWELL 225

I fear nothing so much as a man who is witty all day long.

MADAME DE SÉVIGNÉ

I am one of those unhappy persons who inspire bores to the greatest flights of art.

DAME EDITH SITWELL

Doorman—a genius who can open the door of your car with one hand, help you in with the other, and still have one left for the tip.

DOROTHY KILGALLEN

Don't think it hasn't been charming, because it hasn't.

MARGOT ASQUITH
(to the hostess, upon leaving a party)

Success ────────────────

Success to me is having ten honeydew melons and eating only the top half of each one.

> BARBRA STREISAND

The penalty of success is to be bored by the people who used to snub you.

> NANCY, LADY ASTOR

Success didn't spoil me; I've always been insufferable.

> FRAN LEBOWITZ

The worst part of success is to try finding someone who is happy for you.

> BETTE MIDLER 227

The trouble with the rat race is that even if you win, you're still a rat.

LILY TOMLIN

For some strange reason I can put five bullets into that red thing in the middle of the target.

DR. RUTH WESTHEIMER

Success is counted sweetest
By those who ne'er succeed.

EMILY DICKINSON

Suicide

I don't think suicide is so terrible. Some rainy winter Sunday when there's a little boredom, you should always carry a gun. Not to shoot yourself, but to know exactly that you're always making a choice.

LINA WERTMULLER

Human life consists in mutual service. No grief, pain, misfortune or "broken heart" is excuse for cutting off one's life while any power of service remains. But when all usefulness is over, when one is assured of an unavoidable and imminent death, it is the simplest of human rights to choose a quick and easy death in place of a slow and horrible one.

CHARLOTTE PERKINS GILMAN
(suicide note)

Talk

The telephone is a good way to talk to people without having to offer them a drink.

FRAN LEBOWITZ

[Dr. Samuel] Johnson's conversation was by much too strong for a person accustomed to obsequiousness and flattery; it was mustard in a young child's mouth.

HESTER THRALE

All really great lovers are articulate, and verbal seduction is the surest road to actual seduction.

MARYA MANNES

Most conversations are simply monologues delivered in the presence of a witness.

MARGARET MILLAR

SUFFRAGETTE SERIES Nº 2

ELECTIONEERING

COPYRIGHTED 1909 BY DUNSTON-WEILER LITHOGRAPH CO.

The opposite of talking isn't listening. The opposite of talking is waiting.

FRAN LEBOWITZ

No one really listens to anyone else, and if you try it for a while you'll see why.

MIGNON MCLAUGHLIN

She probably labored under the common delusion that you made things better by talking about them.

DAME ROSE MACAULEY

I'll not listen to reason . . . Reason always means what someone else has got to say.

MRS. GASKELL

If you just say nothing, there is no way they can make you talk.

TWIGGY

Television

Television has proved that people will look at anything rather than each other.

ANN LANDERS

If you read a lot of books, you're considered well-read. But if you watch a lot of TV, you're not considered well-viewed.

LILY TOMLIN

There are days when any electrical appliance in the house, including the vacuum cleaner, seems to offer more entertainment possibilities than the TV set.

HARRIET VAN HORNE

Time

I've been on a calendar, but never on time.

MARILYN MONROE

Five minutes! Zounds! I have been five minutes too late all my life-time!

HANNAH COWLEY

Well, time wounds all heels.

JANE ACE

How much can come
And much can go
And yet abide the World!

EMILY DICKINSON

Travel ─────────

The great and recurring question about abroad is, is it worth getting there?

DAME ROSE MACAULEY

Travel is the most private of pleasures. There is no greater bore than the travel bore. We do not in the least want to hear what he has seen in Hong Kong.

VITA SACKVILLE-WEST

I always say that a girl never really looks as well as she does on board a steamship, or even a yacht.

ANITA LOOS

On a plane you can pick up more and better people than on any other public conveyance since the stagecoach.

ANITA LOOS 235

Traveling is the ruin of all happiness! There's no looking at a building here after seeing Italy.

FANNY BURNEY

Vices ──────────

Small habits, well pursued betimes,
May reach the dignity of crimes.

HANNAH MORE

Between two evils I always pick the one I never tried before.

MAE WEST

Pessimism is a luxury that a Jew can never allow himself.

GOLDA MEIR

Good taste is the worst vice ever invented.

DAME EDITH SITWELL

I have a lust for diamonds, almost like a disease.

ELIZABETH TAYLOR

Cocaine isn't habit-forming. I should know—I've been using it for years.

TALLULAH BANKHEAD

I was not drunk. I was able to speak without the least difficulty initially. I was voluble, even fairly coherent. I experienced a strange kind of mental clarity. My mind seemed to revolve and whirl, like a merry-go-round, I thought, with each turn yielding a brass ring. I was a child again.

GELSEY KIRKLAND
(about cocaine)

One reason I don't drink is that I want to know when I'm having a good time.

NANCY, LADY ASTOR

Even though a number of people have tried, no one has yet found a way to drink for a living.

JEAN KERR 237

One more drink and I'll be under the host.

DOROTHY PARKER

The less I behave like Whistler's mother the night before, the more I look like her the morning after.

TALLULAH BANKHEAD

A little of what you fancy does you good.

MARIE LLOYD

Virtue

Vice is nice
But a little virtue
Won't hurt you.

FELICIA LAMPORT

Virtue has its own reward, but no sale at the box office.

MAE WEST

Every man has been brought up with the idea that decent women don't pop in and out of bed; he has always been told by his mother that "nice girls don't." He finds, of course, when he gets older that this may be untrue; but only in a certain section of society. The great majority of people in England and America are modest, decent and pure-minded and the amount of virgins in the world today is stupendous.

BARBARA CARTLAND

Women's virtue is man's greatest invention.

CORNELIA OTIS SKINNER

No good deed goes unpunished.

CLARE BOOTHE LUCE

If you stop to be kind, you must swerve often from your path.

MARY WEBB 239

War

From the happy expression on their faces, you might have supposed they welcomed the War. I had met people who loved stamps, and men who loved stones and snakes—but I could not imagine any man loving war.

MARGOT ASQUITH

War has . . . become a luxury which only the small nations can afford.

HANNAH ARENDT

War is the unfolding of miscalculations.

BARBARA TUCHMAN

Before a war military science seems a real science, like astronomy. But after a war it seems more like astrology.

DAME REBECCA WEST

You can no more win a war than you can win an earthquake.

JEANNETTE RANKIN

I hated the bangs in the war: I always felt a *silent* war would be more tolerable.

PAMELA HANSFORD JOHNSON

Women ━━━━━━━━━━━━━

The one thing civilization couldn't do anything about—women.

SHELAGH DELANEY

But what is woman?—only one of Nature's agreeable blunders.

HANNAH COWLEY 241

Being a woman is of special interest only to aspiring male transsexuals. To actual women, it is simply a good excuse not to play football.

FRAN LEBOWITZ

The great and almost only comfort about being a woman is that one can always pretend to be more stupid than one is and no one is surprised.

FREYA STARK

It isn't that gentlemen really prefer blondes, it's just that we look dumber.

ANITA LOOS

Women are never stronger than when they arm themselves with their weakness.

MADAME MARIE DU DEFFAND

Women are natural guerrillas. Scheming, we nestle into the enemy's bed, avoiding open warfare, watching the options, playing the odds.

SALLY KEMPTON

I should like to know what is the proper function of women, if it is not to make reasons for husbands to stay at home, and still stronger reasons for bachelors to go out.

GEORGE ELIOT

There are two kinds of women: those who want power in the world, and those who want power in bed.

JACQUELINE KENNEDY ONASSIS

Behind almost every woman you ever heard of stands a man who let her down.

NAOMI BLIVEN

And the crazy part of it was even if you were *clever,* even if you spent your adolescence reading John Donne and Shaw, even if you studied history or zoology or physics and hoped to spend your life pursuing some difficult and challenging career, you *still* had a mind full of all the soupy longings that every high school girl was awash in . . . Underneath it all you longed to be annihilated by love, to be swept off your feet, to be filled up by a giant prick spouting sperm, soapsuds, silks and satins, and, of course, money.

ERICA JONG 243

A woman can look both moral and exciting . . . if she also looks as if it was quite a struggle.

EDNA FERBER

There's a fine line between being sweet and innocent and being a tough broad.

PHYLLIS GEORGE

A woman reading *Playboy* feels a little like a Jew reading a Nazi manual.

GLORIA STEINEM

Women who insist upon having the same options as men would do well to consider the option of being the strong, silent type.

FRAN LEBOWITZ

If you take a woman fishing, it has to be a dull one. Anybody lively scares away the fish. There's a special type of woman, in fact, who is chosen for fishing holidays.

ELIZABETH JENKINS

You don't know a woman until you have had a letter from her.

ADA LEVERSON

I am glad I am not a man, for if I were I should be obliged to marry a woman.

MADAME DE STAËL

Some of us are becoming the men we wanted to marry.

GLORIA STEINEM

Trousers, 1905

Please know that I am aware of the hazards. I want to do it because I want to do it. Women must try to do things as men have tried. When they fail, their failure must be but a challenge to others.

AMELIA EARHART
(in a letter to her husband, before her last flight)

My vigor, vitality and cheek repel me. I am the kind of woman I would run away from.

NANCY, LADY ASTOR

Women's Lib _____

If I were king . . . I would have women participate in all human rights, especially those of the mind. It would seem as if they were born only to deceive—that being the only intellectual exercise allowed them.

MADAME DU CHÂTELET
(1706–1749)

The *divine right* of husbands, like the divine right of kings, may, it is hoped, in this enlightened age, be contested without danger.

MARY WOLLSTONECRAFT
(1759–1797)

The Queen is most anxious to enlist everyone who can speak or write to join in checking this mad, wicked folly of "Woman's Rights" with all its attendant horrors on which her poor, feeble sex is bent, forgetting every sense of womanly feeling and propriety . . . It is a subject which makes the Queen so furious that she cannot contain herself.

QUEEN VICTORIA
(in a letter, 1870)

I can never feel that setting fire to houses and churches and letter-boxes and destroying valuable pictures really helps to convince people that women ought to be enfranchised.

DAME MILLICENT FAWCETT

The argument of the broken pane of glass is the most valuable argument in modern politics.

EMMELINE PANKHURST 247

The history of men's opposition to women's emancipation is more interesting perhaps than the story of that emancipation itself.

VIRGINIA WOOLF

I'm furious about the Women's Liberationists. They keep getting up on soapboxes and proclaiming that women are brighter than men. That's true, but it should be kept very quiet or it ruins the whole racket.

ANITA LOOS

Women's liberation is just a lot of foolishness. It's the men who are discriminated against. They can't bear children. And no one's likely to do anything about that.

GOLDA MEIR

Man is not the enemy here, but the fellow victim. The real enemy is women's denigration of themselves.

BETTY FRIEDAN

... the women's movement hasn't changed *my* sex life. It wouldn't dare.

ZSA ZSA GABOR

I was the first woman to burn my bra . . . it took the fire department four days to put it out!

DOLLY PARTON

A liberated woman is one who has sex before marriage and a job after.

GLORIA STEINEM

During the feminist revolution, the battle lines were again simple. It was easy to tell the enemy, he was the one with the penis. This is no longer strictly true. Some men are okay now. We're allowed to like them again. We still have to keep them in line, of course, but we no longer have to shoot them on sight.

CYNTHIA HEIMEL

. . . the major concrete achievement of the women's movement in the 1970's was the Dutch treat.

NORA EPHRON

Words to Live By ———————

No one can make you feel inferior without your consent.

ELEANOR ROOSEVELT

Always be smarter than the people who hire you.

LENA HORNE

Be plain in dress, and sober in your diet;
In short, my deary, kiss me and be quiet.

LADY MARY WORTLEY MONTAGU

A little credulity helps one on through life very smoothly.

MRS. GASKELL

Saddle your dreams afore you ride 'em.

MARY WEBB

Elegance is refusal.

COCO CHANEL

Expect the worst, and you won't be disappointed.

HELEN MACINNES

Never go to a doctor whose office plants have died.

ERMA BOMBECK

Accept every blind date you can get, even with a girl who wears jeans. Maybe you can talk her out of them.

ABIGAIL VAN BUREN

The biggest sin is sitting on your ass.

FLORYNCE KENNEDY

Fill what's empty. Empty what's full. Scratch where it itches.

ALICE ROOSEVELT LONGWORTH

Keep breathing.

SOPHIE TUCKER 251

Acknowledgments and Dedication

Assembling this book was a delightful but sometimes overwhelming task. I could not have done it without help: from Sharon Nettles, who combines awesome technical skills with an equally impressive sweetness of disposition; from Jerome Leitner and James D. Gordon, who dug through the mists of legal history to track down the Common Scold; from Adrienne Adams, who gave me a day's hard labor; from Madeleine Amgott, who lent me a book; from Cyra McFadden, who mailed me clippings. KBA—Knox Burger, Kitty Sprague, and Kathy Preminger—nursed both me and the project from conception to birth. There are 637 things I could say in praise of humorist and anthologist Robert Byrne, but I'll settle for one: He was unfailingly generous and helpful to a fellow compiler. Most of all, the contribution of my husband, Don Westlake, was and is immeasurable. To all the above, and to the friends and family who offered ideas and encouragement (you know who you are): Thank you.

Finally, to the true authors of this book, from Sappho to Madonna, from Abzug to Zogbaum, this book is gratefully dedicated.

Index

254

261